PIETY AND PERSONALITY

PIETY AND PERSONALITY

THE TEMPERAMENTS OF THE SAINTS

ROSEMARY McGUIRE BERRY

TAN Books
Gastonia, North Carolina

Unless otherwise noted, Scripture quotations are from the Douay-Rheims Bible. Public domain.

Cover design by Jordan Avery

Cover images: *St. Thomas Aquinas* by Alessandro di Mariano di Vanni Filipepi (oil on panel). Bridgeman Images. *The Dream of St. Joseph* by Anton Raphael Mengs. In the Public Domain, via Wikimedia Commons. *Teresa of Ávila* by Peter Paul Rubens (oil on oak wood). In the Public Domain, via Wikimedia Commons. *St. Paul* by Pompeo Girolamo Batoni (oil on canvas). National Trust Photographic Library/John Hammond / Bridgeman Images. *Mary Magdalen with a night light* by Georges de la Tour (oil on canvas). Bridgeman Images. *St. Peter* by Pompeo Girolamo Batoni (oil on canvas). National Trust Photographic Library/John Hammond / Bridgeman Images. Portrait of Sir Thomas More by Hans Holbein the Younger (oil on oak panel). In the Public Domain, via Wikimedia Commons. *St. Therese of Lisieux, 20th century* by F. Roytelet (mural). G. Dagli Orti /© NPL - DeA Picture Library / Bridgeman Images.

Library of Congress Control Number: 2024945027

ISBN: 978–1–5051–3411–7
Kindle ISBN: 978–1–5051–3499–5
ePUB ISBN: 978–1–5051–3498–8

Published in the United States by
TAN Books
PO Box 269
Gastonia, NC 28053
www.TANBooks.com
Printed in India.

"How consoling it is to examine the lives of the saints, and to find them so great, but with natures so similar to our own."

—St. Margaret Mary Alacoque[1]

[1] Pichon, *Seeds of the Kingdom*, 69.

To the person who wrote that most of the saints were Melancholic, which prompted a Sanguine to write a whole book to prove him wrong.

And to my husband and daughters, with unending love.

Contents[2]

[2] Note: Each chapter shines a light on one or two saints in particular, and draws brief examples from other saints like them.

The Choleric Temperament

Choleric [ˈkä-lə-rik, kə'ler-ik] *people are dominant, fearless, and opinionated. Cholerics make the best CEOs; they are born with leadership qualities. They usually see the "big picture" at a glance, and they expect everyone else to see what they see and agree with their plans for what should be done about it. Some of their main strengths are courage, decisiveness, a strong work ethic, and absolute commitment to the goal. Some of their main weaknesses can be bossiness, inclination to anger, lack of pity for those who are seemingly weaker than they are, and willful stubbornness.*

The Melancholic Temperament

Melancholic [me-lən-'kä-lik] *people are idealistic, artistic perfectionists. They pay close attention to details and expect others to do the same. They act from their "gut" or instinct and are strongly influenced by their feelings. Their greatest strengths are their desire to do the right or most perfect thing, their dedication to ideals, and their sympathy toward others. Their weaknesses can be too much perfectionism, indecision because they want to make the perfect decision, and an inclination to depression, often because of too much rumination on their wrongs and disappointments.*

The Sanguine Temperament

Sanguine [saŋ-gwən] *people are impetuous and loving, and they are enthusiastic optimists. Sanguines want to please others and lighten the loads of others with their cheerfulness and spontaneous humor. Their strengths are energy, joy, enthusiasm, positivity, and an inability to bear grudges. Their weaknesses can be instability, inconsistency, and changeability.*

The Phlegmatic Temperament

Phlegmatic [fleg-'ma-tik] *people are imperturbable and peaceful. They avoid conflict, don't seek center stage, and are loyal and loving. Their strengths include sympathy, patience, and calm amidst storms. Their weaknesses can be laziness, stubbornness, and an unwillingness to stand up for the truth because they don't like confrontation.*

Light the Fire: Introduction to the "Why" of this Book

Were the saints *born* holy? Did they pop into the world filled with virtue and sanctity, astounding everyone around them, and putting "normal" people to shame? Some hagiographers (saint-storytellers) would have us believe that, giving accounts of miracles from the cradle, or of astounding acts of penance at two years old. Every saint had to work out his or her salvation. Each saint struggled against his weaknesses and faults; each saint had to plant and cultivate virtue. God's grace is sufficient for every one of us to become great saints.

Yes, you.

And yes, me!

But how?

You may say, "I'm not as brave as St. Isaac Jogues. I'm not as smart as St. Thomas Aquinas. I'm not a world traveler like St. Frances Cabrini." But they did not start out doing amazing things for God. They got there by determined effort and floods of God's grace. Let us take a look at how they did it and see what we can apply to our own lives.

Here. Now. In this modern world.

We can begin by knowing more about ourselves. Fr. Raoul Plus, SJ wrote:

> Who am I? The mystery of each personality! It is a mystery which even the most perfect and most intimate union with another personality cannot completely pierce, as for example in marriage. There is a limitless diversity in personalities, since God made all souls originally without ever copying any previous model . . . Who am I? What are my resources? What are my good points? What are my faults? What is the color of my desires, the force of my will, the intensity of my religious need, my thirst for an integrated life, my Christian fervor, the value of my fidelity?[3]

Saint Augustine, after his conversion, longed to kindle the love of God in his heart. "Let me know Thee who knowest me, let me know Thee even as I am known," he prayed. "I will confess therefore what I know of myself and what I do not know; for what I know of myself I know through the shining of Your light; and what I do not know of myself, I continue not to know until my darkness shall be made as noonday in Your countenance."[4] As a philosopher, he realized that the better he knew himself, the more he could know his Creator. The more we know ourselves, the more we can know, love, and serve God. "Thou shalt love the Lord thy God with thy whole heart" (Matt. 22:37).

"The difficult study of temperament takes for granted an earnest longing after self-perfection," wrote Father Joseph Massmann in his book *Nervousness, Temperament and the Soul.* "The man who is not striving to become a better man resists the truth and keeps out of its way. For those who are

---

3 Plus, *Christ in the Home*, 5.

4 *Confessions*, 173, 176.

striving after inward perfection—even for those who merely want to make a success of life—it is useful, indeed necessary, to examine these questions."[5]

If we study our weaknesses, we can battle them more effectively. If we acknowledge our strengths, we can thank our Maker and work to develop those good tendencies.

The second greatest commandment can also be fulfilled through the study of the human temperament: "Thou shalt love thy neighbor as thyself" (Matt. 22:39). If we comprehend our neighbor's strengths and weaknesses, and why he or she acts and reacts the way they do, we can be more patient and charitable toward them. We can learn to fulfill the needs of others, even if they are different from our own.

Hippocrates, who died c. 375 BC, established the theory of four major personality types and called them the four "humors." He believed that they were caused by an excess of various bodily fluids. Centuries later, scientists of the day commented that when Saint Francis de Sales died, they found a large quantity of excess bile built up in his body. This was believed to have been from his containing his temper and controlling his natural temperament so that he was kind and patient at all times.

As medical science advanced, the discovery was made that a Phlegmatic person did not necessarily have more phlegm in his body, and the Sanguine did not necessarily have more blood than others, but they confirmed that there *are* four distinct classes of people. Understanding these four types—still referred to as Choleric, Sanguine, Melancholic, and Phlegmatic—helps us to comprehend

[5] Massmann, *Nervousness, Temperament and the Soul*, 13.

ourselves and recognize our fellow human beings. Most of us are a combination of at least two temperaments, but many of us have a dominant one.

We might be tempted to think that studying the lives of the saints in order to discover their dominant personality type is inherently difficult because they spent their lives overcoming their weaknesses. It is easy to identify the temperament of someone who is domineering, or ditzy, or lazy, or finicky and hair-splitting; but the saints were not that way!

Or were they?

If we can surmise the probable temperament of, say, a Saint Peter, then we can follow his example in conquering those failings. It is generally accepted that he was of a Sanguine temperament: outgoing, impetuous, excitable, enthusiastic . . . and not terribly consistent or stable. If I have a Sanguine temperament, I can take courage from the story of Saint Peter and see that I, too, can become a great saint.

The Almighty and All-merciful God would not have created a kind of person (Choleric, Sanguine, Melancholic, or Phlegmatic) that could not get to Heaven. He would not have created us with a temperament that was a stumbling-block to our salvation. On the contrary, He gave us exactly the right temperament to *help* us gain Heaven. He placed the right people in our lives, with the right temperaments, to save our souls and everyone around us.

He knows what each soul needs—after all, He created everyone. He knows our strengths and weaknesses, our experiences and knowledge, our joys and our sorrows.

We are not all cookie-cutter images of each other. Our children are not all potatoes that can be cut into matching

French fries of the same size and length. No, rather, every soul is a diocese, as a great saint said. Every soul has heights and depths that we do not know, but God does. Understanding them, and understanding ourselves, is the first key to perfecting ourselves and becoming saints.

If I am a Melancholic mom with a Choleric-Sanguine husband and seven Sanguine children who cannot sit still, cannot stop talking, and cannot remember from one moment to the next what they are supposed to be doing, I will not throw up my hands in despair. God's will is perfect. Maybe I am meant to be the calm, consistent influence in their lives. Maybe they are supposed to be the leaven in my loaf that reminds me that life doesn't always go according to our plans, and that "saints are not sad."

Imagine if everyone in the world was Choleric. Nothing would ever get done because they would all be arguing over the best way to do it, and each would think that he should be the boss. Imagine if the whole world was Melancholic. Since they are perfectionists, nothing would ever be good enough to please all of them, so they would just give up and be depressed. Imagine if the whole world was Phlegmatic. God needn't have bothered to give them free will, because they would rather sleep anyway. And if the whole world was Sanguine, well, they would have a lot of fun, but there would be mass chaos.

The omniscient Creator knew that if He created these four basic types of people, and each person strove to be the best he or she could be, then the world would run like a well-oiled machine: the Cholerics would decide what needed to be done and come up with the perfect plan; the Sanguines would wax enthusiastic and sell the idea to everyone else; the Phlegmatics would quietly do the work, with the Melancholics working alongside and checking to be sure it is done right.

The Master, who made us and redeemed us, is the pinnacle and perfection of all four temperaments. He has the strengths of all four, without any of the weaknesses. He has the decisiveness and farsightedness of a Choleric, joined to the joyfulness and sweetness of a Sanguine, merged with the idealism, diligence, and deep thinking of a Melancholic, with the added peacefulness and patience of a Phlegmatic.

He tells us to take up our cross daily and follow Him (see Luke 9:23). The only way to walk in His footsteps is to keep our eyes on Him and imitate His example. But as I try to follow Him, why am I walking so slowly? Why do I keep tripping and falling?

Let us be conscious of the blister on our left big toe, the old sprain in our right ankle, the twisted knee, aching back, or whatever other "weakness" is slowing us down. The more we identify these deficiencies, the more we can bring them to the Savior to be healed and do the prescribed exercises and physical therapy on them to make those weak points stronger. Maybe we need to shift the cross from our left shoulder to our right shoulder because that is where our strength lies. Understanding our strengths (e.g., forgiving, sympathetic, a good organizer, cheerful, peacemaker) and weaknesses (e.g., forgetfulness, pessimism, over-sensitivity, bossiness) will help us and help those around us.

If I am a religious who feels my superior's temperament is diametrically opposed to mine, I can watch and see what the Master wants me to learn from him or her. If I am a layperson, I can try to discover what He wishes me to learn from my spouse, parents, children, or co-workers. He planted us in this century, in this nation, in this neighborhood, with these particular human beings, and with this temperament, because it would give us, as the individual snowflakes that we are, the best chance to achieve heavenly glory with Him forever.

How can we ever become discouraged with a foundation and support like that? God *believes* in us. He believes that if I use my free will to correspond with His grace, I *will* become a saint. We should have the same confidence that He has. Without Him, we can do nothing. With His grace empowering our free will, we can succeed and become the wonderful people He created us to be.

Ah, but there's the rub, we say. Our free will. It runs away with the passions, like the dish running away with the spoon. Instead of letting our passions elope with our free will, we should strengthen that will, by prayer and effort, to follow our Faith and our reason. Plato called the passions wild, beautiful horses pulling their owner in a chariot. We must keep a firm rein on them and use them to get where we want to go, or they will very easily take flight, with our crazed chariot careening wildly along the path of this life.

Mary Magdalene's life story is a perfect example of this. In the beginning of her life as a Melancholic-Sanguine, her wild horses took her where they pleased, and later, after she met the Master, she learned how to harness their strength and power to take her where she wanted to go—Heaven.

The love of God has been compared to a flame, burning inside the human heart. St. Philip Neri[6] was probably Sanguine, at least partly, and he burned with Divine love. If he *were* Sanguine, it could explain why he avoided women so assiduously, and did most of his work among the men of Rome. He may have been crushing a tendency toward flirtatiousness. Sanguines flirt so easily, they sometimes do it unintentionally. So, he may have been purposely avoiding women because he knew of this natural tendency. Saint Philip's heart was so inflamed with love for God that his body would actually burn up like he had a fever. Let us allow the fire of God's Love to inflame our hearts and brighten our lives with light and warmth.

The flames of the love of God in the Heart of Our Blessed Lady, fueled by the wood of the cross, produced a fragrant incense that enchanted the Most Blessed Trinity. Each of us feeds the flames of love in our hearts with our daily thoughts, words, and actions.

Those of us who are Sanguine might have a tendency to fuel the flame of love with spiritual paper: we flare up dramatically with great sacrifices or great plans or great words, but quickly sputter out into discouragement or changeability. We must learn to cultivate a steadier, more consistent flame.

A visitor to the countryside of Ireland on a spring evening is entranced by the smoky, sweet smell of a turf fire. Like the aroma of a beloved grandfather's pipe, it comforts and warms and tickles the sense of smell. Some Melancholics and Sanguines burn with this kind of steady, fragrant warmth.

---

[6] Saint Philip Neri (1515–1595).

If I am Melancholic or Choleric, I should beware of burning with too high of an intensity, angrily or anxiously feeding my fire in a frenzy to find perfection at my own speed. If we make too extreme of a heat, it will be too much. No one will be able to get close to us because of the fury of our inflammable natures, and we will drive people away.

If I am Phlegmatic, I might find myself lazy or carelessly optimistic in feeding and stoking my fire. We might work for a while and then fizzle out, then procrastinate about finding new fuel, do a little, and fade out again. If those of us who are Phlegmatic are not careful, our ashes may become cold from inactivity and lack of fuel. But virtuous Phlegmatics keep a low, steady flame, from which others can rekindle their own dying embers.

The strongest and most pleasing fire to the Almighty will be the one that is lively, consistent, vigorous, and fueled by the Cross. This will produce the sweetest perfume, the most fragrant incense. Moment by moment, we can feed our daily frustrations, setbacks, disappointments, and trials into the fire of our love for God.

Note: If you are uncertain of your own temperament, do an internet search for the Personality Plus temperament test.

1

Francis de Sales Learns Self-Control

Melancholic-Choleric

This masterful director of souls and brilliant writer of spiritual works was born on August 21, 1567. He was blessed with noble blood, wealth, and a good Catholic family. He was an intellectual genius with a generous heart and a large dose of charm. Like many Cholerics, he probably would have succeeded in any area of life. At the age of thirteen, his father sent him to the University of Paris to help him with worldly success, but Francis chose to enter the Jesuit College. He mastered Greek, Hebrew, and theology and Scripture study. When he was twenty, he entered law school at the University of Padua.

In his biographies, the young man's attention to detail and excellence in every subject lead us to believe that he was a combination of Melancholic and Choleric. Melancholics who are not Choleric are idealistic perfectionists, but do not have the follow-through and stick-to-it-iveness that Melancholic-Cholerics have. At the University of Padua, a favorite professor of St. Francis's was the Jesuit Antonius

Possevinus. He taught the young Francis to meditate according to the method of St. Ignatius of Loyola.

"This method," writes Rev. James F. Cassidy, BA, consists in "making chivalrous devotion to Jesus Christ as King of an army, one of the leading principles designed to direct from above the entire life, emphasizing strictly regulated progress in the conquest of self, and dwelling considerably on detail as making for spiritual enlightenment, proved very attractive to a man profoundly chivalrous, and strictly methodic and thorough in whatever he undertook."[7] One can see how this type of spirituality would have strongly appealed to a Melancholic-Choleric person. St. Ignatius of Loyola, a strong Choleric himself, has much to teach Cholerics down through the ages.

At the age of twenty-four, Francis earned the degree of Doctor of Law, and in 1593, at the age of twenty-six, he was ordained a priest. For the next twenty-nine years, he labored to save souls by uplifting, encouraging, and fortifying them. He became Bishop of Geneva, converted thousands back to the Catholic Faith, and wrote numerous letters and spiritual books which are still in print, over four hundred years later. Most notable among these are his *Introduction to the Devout Life* and *Treatise on the Love of God.* With the help of St. Jane Frances de Chantal, he founded the Order of Visitation nuns. He departed this life for Heaven on December 28, 1622, at the age of fifty-five.

"Everything in this admirable Saint enchants and fascinates us," writes Father Gaspar Gilli, "Whoever reads his writings

[7] Cassidy, *St. Francis de Sales*, 13.

attentively, feels constrained, not only to honor and venerate him, but also to love him."[8]

Yet his gentleness did not come naturally to him. It is said that when someone asked him why he did not show his frustration with a certain difficult boatman, Francis admitted to those closest to him, "I am afraid to lose in a quarter of an hour that little sweetness which I have gathered up, drop by drop, like dew in the vessel of my heart, through the efforts of twenty years." In other words, he had worked so hard to gain his meekness that he was afraid if he let the wild horses have their heads, his anger would rage out of control. This can also be compared to an alcoholic person who knows he shouldn't take a single sip of an alcoholic drink, because he knows his weakness.

> ***Tip for Cholerics:*** *Fight for patience and meekness in hand-to-hand combat with yourself—moment by moment, hour by hour.*

Meekness is a much-misunderstood virtue. It does not mean mousiness, lack of courage, or making oneself a doormat. It is the opposite of anger, the opposing virtue to the capital sin of anger. Our Lord Jesus Christ exemplified meekness when He patiently suffered His Passion, instead of destroying His persecutors with a lightning bolt.

St. Francis de Sales is often quoted to have said, "Nothing is so strong as gentleness, nothing so gentle as real strength."

By nature, Francis de Sales possessed a fiery temperament, but by prolonged efforts, he has become a saint renowned through the centuries as a saint of sweetness and consolation, placing countless souls on the way of perfection. He determined never to speak when he was upset. What a courageous resolution for a Choleric to make!

---

[8] Gilli, *The Month of Mary*, preface.

"It is a difficult task to preserve peace in the soul, and well he knew it," continues Father Gilli. "St. Francis acquired all his benignity, fighting for it, we may say, hand to hand against his natural impetuosity. This virtue by degrees penetrated the inmost parts of his soul, so that it was not only manifested in all the actions of his life, but it directed also his pen."[9]

He fought against his temper and his own sharp wit—the man was brilliant and highly educated—moment by moment, thought by thought, word by word. St. Francis de Sales is famous for telling the faithful that if we fall, we must jump right up again and keep trying. He spoke from his own experience.

Sigrid Undset writes in her life of another Choleric—*Catherine of Siena*[10]—thus: "[Her family] could not help noticing at home that Catherine became more and more patient and calm. Many years later she came to call patience the very marrow of piety, and in view of the fact that grace does not alter our inborn nature, but perfects it, one must believe that this young woman who was later, with such awe-inspiring energy and whole-heartedness, to do all that her visions told her was God's will, must have been born with an unusual reserve of natural willfulness."[11]

Tip for Cholerics: *Make a determined act of your powerful will: I will become a saint!*

Catherine used her strong will in the direction of cultivating meekness and patience. Once a Choleric's will is turned and tuned to God's will, he or she can do great things because of this "natural willfulness" and tenacious

---

[9] Gilli, *The Month of Mary*, preface.

[10] Saint Catherine of Siena (1347–1380).

[11] Undset, *Catherine of Siena*, 17.

concentration on the final goal. The Choleric can and will conquer his shortcomings once he is convinced of their existence—sometimes that is the tricky part. Whether they are courting their future spouse or starting a company, whether they are scrubbing the floor or starting a Catholic youth group, Cholerics are almost always successful once they set their mind to something.

Marcelle Auclair describes St. Teresa of Ávila's work to overcome her Choleric-Sanguine weaknesses: "She knew for the future that feelings, desires, wishes, attitudes, that which can form our character and yet is nothing but a collection of tendencies which practice and habit can overcome or develop, are under the control of the will. God created man free to choose perfection." Then she quotes the saint herself as saying, "This act of the will (*determinacion* in her native Spanish) is what He wants."[12]

> ***Tip for all Temperaments:*** *Understanding our temperament and our weaknesses is the first step. Then use them as a springboard to "choose perfection," as Marcelle Auclair says, and work toward it.*

Understanding our temperament and our weaknesses is the first step. The next step is to realize that our temperament is not an *excuse* but a springboard. Beginning with a knowledge of these strengths and these weaknesses, we can "choose perfection," as Marcelle Auclair wrote above, and work toward it.

When we study the life and words of Saint Francis de Sales, the temperament we see *least* in him is Choleric. We see the friendliness of the Sanguine, the unflappability of the Phlegmatic, and the intuition and empathy of the

---

[12] Auclair, *Saint Teresa of Avila*, 35. Saint Teresa of Ávila was born in 1515 and died in 1582.

Melancholic. He desires perfection like a Melancholic, he finds peace like a Phlegmatic, and he loves like a Sanguine.

The only Choleric quality we still see in the Bishop of Geneva is his clinging to the objective despite all odds. He made a choice of will (Teresa's *determinacion*) and stuck to it even if it meant crushing his natural tendencies—*especially* if it meant crushing his natural tendencies—to become what God wanted him to be. His personal plans for sanctity sound like someone with a strong dose of both Choleric and Melancholic. For instance, he wrote out what he was going to do if this or that happened, what he would say or do if he met this difficult person, and what he would do if he encountered this or that particular temptation. Cholerics are good at making plans, and Melancholics are good at details.

St. Francis de Sales was gentle and kind to all. To find Christian perfection, the saint built on his innate tendencies. He cultivated the strengths of the Sanguine, like sweetness, warmth, and affability, and those of the Phlegmatic, like calmness, patience, and gentleness. Father Hock, in his book, *The Four Temperaments*, even opines that this saint was Sanguine by nature.[13]

The fact that Francis made lists of specific ways to avoid imperfections, faults and sins, and lists of possible temptations and ways to avoid them leads us to think that he was more Melancholic. We will have to ask Bishop de Sales when we get to Heaven. The fact remains that he worked so hard at the strengths of the four temperaments, and battled so bravely against the weaknesses, that he provides an excellent

---

[13] Hock, *The Four Temperaments*, 11.

example of self-mastery to all of us, no matter what our temperament might be.

When he co-founded the Order of the Visitation with St. Jane Frances de Chantal,[14] he made meekness its heart. Monseigneur Bougaud, in his wondrous two-volume work, *St. Chantal and the Foundation of the Visitation*, compares the Visitation nuns with two other major orders popular in the 17th century. He talks about the charity of St. Vincent de Paul's[15] Daughters of Charity, and the spirit of penance of the Carmelites, as reformed by St. Teresa of Ávila. St. Francis and St. Jane, however, gave the Visitandines a different focal point.

"The daughter of St. Francis de Sales," writes Monseigneur Bougaud, "immolates herself by interior sacrifice, and by her attention to maintaining herself recollected, meek, humble, amiable, and agreeable to all and at all times . . . Her distinctive characteristic is meekness."[16]

Meekness is an attractive virtue. A person who never loses their temper often has many friends. "The patient man is better than the valiant: and he that ruleth his spirit than he that taketh cities" (Prov. 16:32). St. Vincent de Paul said that a meek superior is one who is obeyed. His or her good temper makes others want to follow and obey.

Our Lord showed His meekness time and again in His public life. When a Samaritan town would not let Him enter, James and John, the "Sons of Thunder," (Mark 3:17)

---

[14] Saint Jane Frances de Chantal (1572–1641).

[15] Saint Vincent de Paul (1581–1660).

[16] Bougaud, *St. Chantal and the Foundation*, vol. 1, 37.

asked Him, "Lord, wilt thou that we command fire to come down from heaven, and consume them?" (Luke 9:54).

But He turned and rebuked them, saying, "You know not of what spirit you are. The Son of man came not to destroy souls, but to save" (Luke 9:55–56). Who has more authority than Jesus Christ? And yet He was meek. Many Cholerics in authority have a tendency to "lord it over" others. Let us learn from the meek Savior and His followers how to treat others.

St. Alphonsus de Ligouri[17] often talks about and quotes St. Francis de Sales. He writes: "St. Francis of Sales says that nothing edifies our neighbor so much as meekness in our conduct. Hence everything in him partook of this beautiful virtue; his air, his words, his manners, all was meekness . . . If he was obliged in conscience to refuse any favor, he accompanied the refusal with so much charity, that the unsuccessful applicant went away satisfied."[18]

Tip for Cholerics: *Who has more authority than Jesus Christ? Yet He was meek. Let us learn from Him and His followers how to treat others.*

St. Alphonsus goes on to talk about how the best corrections (of a supervisor to an employee, a superior to a nun or priest, a parent to a teenager, etc.) are made with meekness. He says that St. Vincent de Paul only made three "severe reprimands" in his life, and he regretted them, because they were unsuccessful. Meekness has a much greater success rate in achieving the goal of correcting someone and guiding their behavior in a new direction.

We talked about "lighting the fire" in the introduction, but there is more than one type of fire. St. Alphonsus writes,

[17] Saint Alphonsus de Ligouri (1696–1787).

[18] de Ligouri, *Love of Our Lord*, 54.

"St. Bernard[19] observes, that there are some who are affable and meek only as long as things go on according to their wishes; but if a contradiction, or a cross befall them, they are immediately inflamed, and emit smoke like Mount Vesuvius; they resemble burning coals, that are concealed under ashes."[20] A man or a woman such as St. Bernard describes quite literally "blows their top" like a volcanic eruption. Though a person of any temperament can have a temper, Cholerics are prone to this. Therefore, wise and prudent Cholerics will cultivate meekness.

"The heart of the wise shall instruct his mouth; and shall add grace to his lips. Well ordered words are as a honeycomb: sweet to the soul, and health to the bones" (Prov. 16:23–24).

As we said, meekness attracts people. St. Gregory Nazianzen[21] said that his contemporary St. Athanasius[22] was a magnet to the hesitant. These words can, with equal accuracy, be applied to St. Francis de Sales. He converted tens of thousands of Calvinists back to the Catholic Faith. He drew souls with his magnetic personality. Want to know his secret? In addition to his meekness, he truly loved the souls of others and wanted to help them. They felt this and were imperceptibly pulled toward him and what he taught.

By the end of his life, he had become what we all aspire to be, a reflection of his Master, Our Lord Jesus Christ. St. Vincent de Paul, a contemporary of St. Francis who knew him in life, said "that he never knew any man more meek;

---

19 Saint Bernard of Clairvaux (1090–1153).

20 de Ligouri, 58–59.

21 Saint Gregory Nazianzen (329–390 AD).

22 Saint Athanasius (c. 296–373 AD).

and added, that he seemed to find him the living image of the meekness of our Savior."[23]

Katherine F. Mullany, in her short work, *Miriam of Magdala: a Study*, draws a vivid word picture of the people witnessing Our Lord's death on Calvary and how they felt about Him. Just as St. Vincent de Paul was reminded of Our Lord's love and gentleness by St. Francis de Sales, we are reminded of what grace and effort wrought in Francis's soul by meditating on this scene of Our Lord's life. Thus, we learn from the lives of the saints. They are like rainbow reflections from the sparkling crystal of Our Lord's own life. Each saint reflects a different color of the prism.

> ***Tip for All Temperaments:*** *We learn from the lives of the saints. They are like rainbow reflections from the sparkling crystal of Our Lord's own life. Each saint reflects a different color of the prism.*

Here is Katherine Mullany's reflection on how the disciples on Calvary saw Him: "[He had been] the sweetest influence their lives had ever experienced; the consoler of their sorrows; the healer of all their ills. His preaching had lifted their souls heavenwards in holy aspirations; His teaching had softened hearts, and sweetened minds, and smoothed away difficulties between friends. Never had His Lips uttered aught but kindly words; never were His deeds but those of love and mercy. In His footsteps sprang up blessings for those who followed Him. His time was given to them without limit, and none there were, who appealed to Him for help in vain."[24]

Think of the Cholerics you know, or perhaps of the Choleric side of your own temperament. Can you imagine these

---

[23] de Ligouri, 55.

[24] Mullany, *Miriam of Magdala*, 88.

words being applied to the Cholerics you know? Or to yourself? Ah, but God's grace can work great wonders in a soul, if we are willing to work with His grace and overcome our weaknesses and unworthy tendencies!

Twenty-five years after the death of St. Francis de Sales, St. Margaret Mary Alacoque[25] was born. This well-known visionary who was privileged to see the Sacred Heart of Jesus and receive the revelation of the First Fridays, became a Visitation nun, and therefore a spiritual daughter of St. Francis de Sales. Father Jean Croiset, SJ (1656–1738), wrote a small introductory biography of Saint Margaret Mary Alacoque in his spiritual classic *The Devotion to the Sacred Heart of Our Lord Jesus Christ.* Like the sainted founder of her order, she learned to control and harness her passions.

"Her meekness and evenness of temper were all the more admirable because they did not proceed from her natural disposition;" wrote Father Croiset. "She had acquired this admirable tranquility of soul by constant vigilance over herself, by constant interior mortification, and especially by continuous union with God; and grace elevated her to such a high degree of peace and evenness of spirit that she was proof against all the vicissitudes and occupations of life."[26]

It is easy to think that if we could just keep from blowing our top, we would be showing perfect meekness. Remember, meekness is neither mousiness nor inactivity. Meekness is the strong virtue that is opposed to anger.

Our Lord said, "Learn of me, because I am meek, and humble of heart" (Matt. 11:29). Our Lord certainly wasn't a weak

---

[25] Saint Margaret Mary Alacoque (1647–1690).

[26] Croiset, *Devotion to the Sacred Heart*, 7.

man, a doormat, or a spineless sissy. And neither were any of the saints. Meekness, especially in a Choleric, is the result of untiring effort and intrepid courage in the face of battling the greatest enemy of all—our own self-love and failings. Simply being quiet when we want to rant and rage is not enough, either. Seething inside while not vocalizing it is not true meekness.

"The first degree of the virtue of meekness is to give no outward token of anger, by sign, by word, or by action," wrote Father Collins in 1880.[27]

This is not a mastery of meekness; it is merely the first step. Father Collins continues, "The second degree [of meekness] is to hold one's spirit in sweet peace within when thwarted . . . and the third degree is to rejoice at tribulations, and to find in crosses a sweet hidden manna."[28]

Tip for Cholerics:* *Comprehend and cultivate true meekness.

St. Francis de Sales accomplished this third degree of meekness. He became so peaceful and calm amid frustrations and disappointments that people felt they had to ask, "Aren't you going to tell him off?" That is when he explained that it had taken him years to be able to greet such occasions with tranquility, and he was not about to "blow it" now.

Francis often told his spiritual children, "Ask for nothing, refuse nothing."[29] This spirit of maintaining peace of soul, and accepting what God sends in His perfect providence and wisdom, gave the two saints—Francis de Sales and Jane de Chantal—and their disciples an enviable tranquility.

---

[27] Collins, *Heaven Opened*, 176.

[28] Collins, 176.

[29] Bougaud, *St. Chantal and the Foundation*, vol. 2, 168.

God often uses peace of soul to communicate with us. In this crazy world, filled with distractions and noise, with endless chatter in our own heads and the din of the electronics which surround us and enter our minds via electronic wireless devices imbedded in our ears, sometimes we forget the importance of slowing down to listen.

Listen.

To what?

To God.

Are we restless? Are we in inner turmoil?

The answer is meditation with the one true God. The devil does not want us to examine the state of our soul, heart, and mind. He wants us to keep a mad, restless, careening pace through life. Then, if we do crave peace and quiet, some people turn to something like yoga or zen that empties the intellect and makes the mind blank, but that has been known to invite the devil to enter and possess that space. "And when an unclean spirit is gone out of a man he walketh through dry places seeking rest, and findeth none. Then he saith: I will return into my house from whence I came out. And coming he findeth it empty, swept, and garnished. Then he goeth, and taketh with him seven other spirits more wicked than himself, and they enter in and dwell there: and the last state of that man is made worse than the first. So shall it be also to this wicked generation" (Matt. 12:43–45).

> ***Tip for All Temperaments:*** *True Catholic meditation fills the soul with the fragrant sweetness of God, thoughts of God, movements of love for God, and conversation with God. This kind of meditation brings deep peace and tranquility.*

So instead of emptying our souls and making them blank, let us fill our hearts with God. Each time we do an act of love while in the state of sanctifying grace (e.g., saying a prayer, attending Mass, going to Confession, showing kindness to someone, fulfilling our daily duties for His glory), we add drops of perfume to our soul. True Catholic meditation fills the soul with the fragrant sweetness of God, thoughts of God, movements of love for God, and conversation with God. This kind of meditation brings deep peace and tranquility.

Now and again, we should take inventory of our internal supplies. Are we depleted by sins, faults, and complaints? Are we collecting bits of honey drop by drop to fill up our soul with His love and His grace, like St. Francis de Sales? If we do, we will find peace: a little taste of the peace of the hereafter—forever with Him.

We should not permit the devil to make so much noise that we cannot grasp the truth. Sometimes he just makes a lot of disturbance and distraction and distress just for the heck of it, and our soul is doing just fine! (Notice how all those "d" words begin with the same letter as "devil.") A good spiritual director and a devout Ignatian retreat can help us to tell the difference.

The devil brings sadness, despair, negativity, dissatisfaction, and irritation wherever he goes. He cannot help himself. Those emotions linger around him like a cloud of acrid smoke. When we feel these negative feelings, whether it is the sadness and depression that Melancholics are prone to, or the anger and hostility that Cholerics are prone to, let us turn to God instead.

The peace, quiet, and sweet contentment to be found in the Holy Sacrifice of the Mass in a Traditional Catholic Church is something the devil hates. The endless chatter, raucous music, and handshaking of more modern ceremonies do not offer this silence. Maybe that is why the lines for the Sacrament of Penance are so short these days. No one has a quiet moment (even in church) to examine one's soul.

Some believe that meditation is only for mystics, those who have ecstasies, raptures, and who are "caught up to the third heaven," like St. Paul (2 Cor. 12:2). Our friend, the Choleric Saint Teresa of Ávila, tells us that it is not only accessible but necessary.

> ***Tip for Cholerics:*** *Find inner peace through Catholic meditation, spiritual direction, and if possible, a retreat.*

"She assures us," writes St. Alphonsus, "That the reason why the devil makes such efforts to withdraw our souls from meditation, is because he knows that he has no chance of gaining the soul which perseveres in this holy exercise."[30]

St. Alphonsus, St. Ignatius,[31] St. Francis de Sales, and St. Teresa, all offer step-by-step instructions on how to achieve meditation on the things of God. Though it takes practice, it is not as hard as it sounds. St. Alphonsus admonishes, "He who does not meditate on eternal truths cannot, without a miracle, lead a Christian life, because, without meditation, he is without light, and walks in darkness."[32] There is that image of fire again. Fire brings warmth and light. "My heart grew hot within me: and in my meditation a fire shall flame out" (Ps. 38:4). Instead of a flaming volcano of rage, let us enkindle the fire of love of God through meditation.

---

30 de Ligouri, *The Love of Our Lord*, 80.

31 Saint Ignatius of Loyola (1491–1556).

32 de Ligouri, 79.

St. Francis de Sales wrote his famous *Introduction to the Devout Life* specifically for laypeople. In it, he describes the process of meditation. He begins by instructing us to place ourselves in the Presence of God mentally. We can think of Him as present everywhere, as present specifically in our soul, in His humanity looking down from Heaven, or as a man standing beside us. The best method for you is whichever of these moves your heart the most.

The next step, St. Francis tells us, is to call upon God with "short, burning words."[33] "Oh God, have mercy on me, a sinner. Oh my Lord, I love Thee." The Psalms are full of such words of love and fervor. The saint also suggests that we call upon Our Lady and the angels and saints to help us in our meditation, especially those who are connected to the topic of our meditation that day.

Step three is to begin thinking about the subject you have chosen. Are you drawn to the mystery of Christmas—God born in a stable for love of you? Is it more appealing to you to think of the Savior treading the dusty roads of the Holy Land on His tired sandaled feet, preaching and healing the multitudes? Maybe you are more moved to contemplate His silent, obscure life, when He spent thirty years learning a carpenter's trade and not revealing His true identity. Perhaps the earth-quaking event of the Resurrection inspires your heart with faith and joy. Whatever you choose, imagine the mystery.

St. Francis says, "By means of the imagination we confine our mind within the mystery on which we meditate, that it may not ramble to and fro, just as we shut up a bird in a cage

---

33 de Sales, *Introduction to the Devout Life*, 82.

or tie a hawk by his leash so that he may rest on the hand."[34] Using our imagination to picture Our Lord or His Mother in some mystery like this helps us to concentrate.

The fourth step is to understand what we are seeing in our imagination. Dwell on it; think about it; place yourself there. Absorb what you are seeing.

The fifth step is to move our hearts toward what God wants us to learn from this. "Yet you must not dwell upon these general reflections," says St. Francis, "without determining to reduce them to special and particular resolutions for your own correction and amendment."[35] Basically, in lay terms, "Now what are you going to do about it?" Christ died on the Cross for you: What are you going to do about it?

Finally, we make acts of thanksgiving, offering, and supplication. We've made our resolutions, now we finish with a short vocal prayer.

"Besides all of this," he concludes, "You must gather a little devotional bouquet. This is what I mean. Those who have been walking in a beautiful garden do not willingly depart without gathering in their hands four or five flowers to smell and keep for the rest of the day. Thus ought we . . . to select one or two or three of those points in which we have found most relish and which are most proper for our advancement, to think frequently on them, and to smell them spiritually during the course of the day."[36]

The habit of daily meditation will do wonders for our meekness and peace of soul. Physical exercise on a regular

---

[34] de Sales, 83.

[35] de Sales, 85.

[36] de Sales, 86.

basis, in the temporal realm, keeps us strong in our bodies. Meditation with God makes our souls strong in the spiritual life and brings us peace.

True peace cannot coexist with evil. Peace and love, contrary to the 1960s moral revolution, do not equal tolerance of the devil, his works, and his pomps. We are the Church Militant. Often, the battle will rage around us externally, but we seek true peace of the soul. Storms of persecution, suffering, misunderstandings, sickness, death, worry, and anxiety will blow; however, we can look inward and focus on a well-formed conscience, solid principles of Catholic teaching, and wise, prudent spiritual direction from a Traditional Catholic priest.

Tip for All Temperaments: *We cannot guide a soul until we love that soul, and until that soul* ***knows*** *that and* ***feels*** *loved by us.*

When I say that storms and battles will rage around us, I do not mean that we should conflict with others through our own fault. Many Catholics nowadays go around with their "dukes up" looking for an argument or a fight. The saints did not seek conflict. We cannot convert people to the one true Faith by hitting them over the head with it. Let us share joyfully and peacefully when we have the opportunity, but not cause rancor, distrust, and conflict between Catholics and non-Catholics, and between Catholics and Catholics.

Even among Catholics, we are not all on the same page at the same time. Maybe you can see clearly the imprudence, vanity, or worldliness of your Catholic neighbor, but it does not necessarily mean that it is your job to tell him so. We should only admonish the erring when we have peace of soul ourselves, like Francis de Sales did.

One time, he attended a sermon in which the priest was scolding because more people had not come. St. Francis said afterward the equivalent of, "What was he yelling at us for? We were there. Did he want us to split ourselves into pieces to fill the empty pews?"[37] In his witty way, he was teasing that riding, berating, and scolding souls does not appeal to them and help them on the way to sanctity. He advised others that we cannot guide a soul until we love that soul, and until that soul *knows* that and *feels* loved by us.

Tip for Cholerics: *We should only admonish the erring when we have peace of soul ourselves, like Francis de Sales did.*

If we have faults and shortcomings, (which of course, we do, there is no doubt about that), how do we want others to show *us* the error of our ways? Do we want them to criticize us or tear us down? No, we want them to show that they care about our well-being by loving us, praying for us, and then only saying something at a time that we are open to hear it and ready to change. When our hearts are filled with Christ's own peace and love, and we feel that the person who is speaking truly cares about us, then we can be amenable to their input.

Let us seek the red rose of true charity, and the white rose of God's peace of soul, instead of sticky-sweet, cheap drugstore perfume that is supposed to smell like roses. None of that cheap, fake stuff for us.

Let us speak kindly and patiently to others like St. Francis de Sales, rather than charging around on our high horses, telling everyone what they are doing wrong and how they ought to fix it. Otherwise, we may find ourselves, like Saint Paul, being "knocked off our high horse."

---

[37] See Roche, *A Bedside Book of Saints*, 75.

2

Conversion of Saint Paul

Choleric

St. Paul (originally named Saul) was born in Tarsus, in present-day Turkey. He was a tentmaker by trade, a Jew by religion, and a Roman by citizenship. He lived sixteen-hundred years before St. Francis de Sales. We first hear of him in Sacred Scripture in Acts, after the Ascension of Our Lord.

We read in the account of the death of St. Stephen, the first martyr for the Faith: "And casting him forth without the city, they stoned him; and the witnesses laid down their garments at the feet of a young man, whose name was Saul" (Acts 7:57). We learn clearly: "And Saul was consenting to his death" (Acts 7:59). The Holy Ghost, through the Scripture, reveals that Saul was not an innocent bystander. He knew what was happening and was an accessory because he watched the killers' coats for them while they did the deed.

In chapter nine of the Acts of the Apostles, Saul's name emerges again with a vengeance: "And Saul, as yet breathing out threatenings and slaughter against the disciples of the Lord, went to the high priest, and asked of him letters to Damascus, to the synagogues: that if he found any men and women of this way, he might bring them bound to Jerusalem" (Acts 9:1–2).

Cholerics like St. Paul have great initiative and are moved by strong emotions and beliefs. They see the big picture and often generalize. He despised all Catholics and acted on his convictions. He wanted to be the one to bring the "rebels" back to Jerusalem in chains. Our Lord's personal encounter with this vigorous, hard-riding, bull-headed Roman citizen is a beautiful part of Church history.

As Saul rode at a full gallop in the direction he thought was right, he was thrown from his horse and blinded by a flash of light. Our Lord spoke to him: "Saul, Saul, why persecutest thou Me?" (Acts 9:4). Saul, who had been chasing followers of "that Nazarene," learned that Our Lord thought of His disciples as part of Himself. The direct approach was the only one that would work with this Choleric, and Our Lord knew that, of course.

After three days of darkness and prayer, Jesus sent Ananias to Paul to baptize him. As hard as he had stormed in one direction, he now charged in the opposite one. Rev. Richard Brennan, in his *A History of the Catholic Church*, writes: "With what astonishment and chagrin the Jews in Damascus looked upon this once bigoted Pharisee and bitter foe of Christianity, as he went into their synagogue, and with superhuman eloquence preached that the crucified Nazarite was the veritable Messias!"[38]

Like St. John the Baptist, Saul retired to the desert to connect with God and ascertain his mission. When he returned,

---

[38] Brennan, *History of the Catholic Church*, 34.

he was on fire with faith and charity. The number of miles he traveled preaching the Gospel is astonishing.

He went to Antioch in AD 45. and journeyed for four years through Cyprus and Asia Minor. In the year AD 51, he attended the Council of the Apostles in Jerusalem, and then headed back to Asia Minor, then Macedonia and Greece, for another two years. From AD 54 to 58, he preached in Ephesus, Macedonia, Illyria, and Greece. When he returned to Jerusalem, he was imprisoned for two years. He appealed to the Roman government because of his citizenship and was transferred to Rome where he was incarcerated for two more years.

When he was freed, he went to Spain and returned to some of his other missions. Eventually, he went back to Rome with St. Peter around the year AD 67 where he was imprisoned again. The two were jailed at the Mamertine Prison together, until Peter was crucified and Paul, as a Roman citizen, was beheaded.

Cholerics are often self-generated and self-motivated; they instinctively make the right decision, without delay, and move forward with no doubts as to their own wisdom. Dazzling bursts of certainty provide the light for their discernments and determinations. We see this in the story of St. Paul, the quintessential Choleric apostle. He rode at a full gallop to Damascus, ready to imprison all the Christians he could find, for not agreeing with what he thought was the right religion. His zeal and absolute conviction of his rectitude guided him unfalteringly. Cholerics are sure of their facts, even when they are dead wrong.

Florence Littauer, a temperaments expert, wrote, "[A Choleric] speaks in absolutes and tends to look at others as if they were prize dummies. It is better not to disagree with him in a social situation for he loves to argue, and he will prove you wrong even if you are right. You will find it difficult to escape from his proof, and he may follow you to the car, expounding his logic until you dutifully agree that black is white."[39]

As Saint Paul (then known as Saul of Tarsus) spurred his horse to ever greater speeds in his mission, Our Lord Jesus Christ knocked him off his high horse. Paul could have said, "It came to me in a blinding flash." In an actual flash of light that physically blinded him, Our Lord threw him from his horse and enlightened Saul the tentmaker (see Acts 9:3–9).

Cholerics need a head-on approach. They often do not comprehend subtleties and niceties. We talked earlier about only offering fraternal correction when the person is ready to receive it, but when it is time to correct a Choleric, we need to be direct. They are not afraid of conflict: many of them revel in it. Of course, standing up to them when they are angry should only be done when necessary. In general, greater success is achieved by waiting until the Choleric is in a calm, receptive mood.

Even after Saul converted and became Paul the Apostle, his reformed but still present temperament shows in his epistles. The attitude, "I can do anything; I'm invincible," changed to, "I can do all these things in Him Who strengtheneth me" (Phil. 4:13). He learned to lean on Christ, instead of his own strength. When he knew that his martyrdom was approaching,

[39] Littauer, *Personality Plus,* 167.

he wrote with humble confidence, "I have fought a good fight, I have finished my course, I have kept the Faith" (2 Tim. 4:7).

A Choleric does not lose the strengths of his temperament when he is sanctified; instead, his greatest attributes are transformed. If St. Paul had not been a Choleric, filled with determination and zeal, he would not have been able to travel the many miles, suffer the numerous hardships, and convert so many to the cause of Christ.

A monk once said of Cholerics in a profound summation, "They're either out there converting nations or they're criminal masterminds."[40] There is nothing in between for this temperament. So, if you are a Choleric, or someone close to you is, the decision has to be made: choose your side.

Tip for Cholerics: *Make a choice—God or mammon? You won't lose your edge; it will be uplifted and sanctified!*

"Deep and passionate temperaments which either are not trained or are left to themselves," wrote Father Joseph Massmann, "rage like torrents and leave in their path a sort of devastation."[41] Instead of sweeping through life leaving destruction behind them, Cholerics must learn self-control and use their leadership tendencies to blaze a trail of virtue and lead the charge to Heaven.

"An utter humiliation might save their souls, as a last chance," writes W. H. Anderdon, SJ, "A powerful whisper may make itself heard in their hearts; or a flash of revealed majesty smite them in mid-career: 'Saul, Saul, why dost thou persecute Me?' And we would, please God, be very far from the reserved and doubtful spirit of Ananias, could we

---

[40] Private correspondence with author.

[41] Massmann, *Nervousness, Temperament and the Soul*, 14.

but once hear them cry out, humbled and penitent, 'Lord, what wouldst Thou have me do?'"[42]

God assigned Ananias to instruct Paul, but Ananias expressed doubt. In modern parlance, he said the equivalent of, "Wait, what? Saul of Tarsus? Are you sure about that, Lord?"

What diverted Paul from his mad track of vengeance? Our Divine Lord knew that he was capable of great things, with his forceful personality, his courage, his leadership abilities, and his fearless zeal. Jesus had great plans for this Choleric. First, He knocked him down and blinded him in order to teach him humility, and then He told him to go into Damascus and wait for further instructions (see Acts 9:7).

Whoa! Blind obedience *and* patient waiting? Our Lord was asking a lot of someone with Paul's temperament. But Paul had been convinced. He did not understand it yet, but he now knew that he had to change.

After three days of persevering prayer and self-examination on Saul's part, Our Lord sent Ananias to help, heal, and baptize Saul, whose Roman name was Paul. Our Lord said, "Arise, and go into the street that is called Strait, and seek . . . one named Saul of Tarsus. For behold he prayeth" (Acts 9:11). Isn't that line profound? Our Lord sent His messenger to Paul because "he prayeth." It may not be easy for a Choleric to humble himself to regular prayer.

"A short but fervent prayer will usually do more to bring about a conversion than long discussions or fine speeches," writes Dom Chautard in his spiritual classic, *The Soul of the*

---

[42] Anderdon, *Afternoons with the Saints*, 14.

Apostolate.[43] St. Stephen's fervent prayer of forgiveness for Saul and the others who brought about his martyrdom, "Lord, lay not this sin to their charge!" (Acts 7:59), quite possibly brought about the conversion of one of the greatest evangelizers the Catholic Church has ever known. Of course, since Saul was Choleric, Our Lord had to do something drastic to bring the answer to Stephen's prayer.

Tip for Cholerics: *Pray with your whole heart!*

Regular personal prayer is essential to every soul, and not just a Choleric's sturdy recitation of the family Rosary, while forcing his children to participate. Words like these might be heard: "Kneel up! Stop jiggling your rosary beads! I can't hear you! Speak up!" The family Rosary is a beautiful devotion that should embellish every Catholic home, but it is not the only way to honor God. A Choleric should make the time to pray personally to God in a one-on-one, unrehearsed conversation, and as we discussed previously, take time for Catholic meditation. One of the greatest experts on mental prayer is our next Choleric saint: Teresa of Ávila.

When a Choleric is converted, he or she must avoid another pitfall. The great Chautard writes, "To hear these mighty men [or women] of works talking about their exploits, one might imagine that God Almighty, to Whom it is child's play to create worlds, and before Whom the universe is dust and nothingness, cannot get along without their cooperation;"[44] and further . . . "Full steam ahead! And while the helmsman is admiring the rapidity of his progress, God sees that, since the pilot does not know his job, the ship is

---

43 Chautard, *Soul of the Apostolate*, 36.

44 Chautard, 25.

off the course and is in danger of being wrecked."[45] In other words, the Choleric, who was first charging confidently in the wrong direction, may wheel his figurative horse and ride even more confidently too far in the other direction.

The answer, once again, is found in those simple words of Our Lord to Ananias, Go to him because "he prayeth."

Dom Chautard says that some (probably Choleric) people would much prefer long hours of work in the field (or office) to half an hour of mental prayer or an attentive assisting at daily Mass. Our Lord gives us the answer: "We ought always to pray, and not to faint" (Luke 18:1).

When Paul's prayer life increased, and he stopped following his own will long enough to hear what God was saying to him, he began to traverse the long road to personal greatness and high levels of sanctity.

Once Cholerics are convinced of what must be done, they are committed and consistent. They are decisive and determined. The Choleric does not know how to be wishy-washy or lazy, or how to do things in half-measures. Once he or she is convinced of the necessity and righteousness of a certain action (even when misguided), he or she will stand by it to the death. This is their strength, which can be used for good or for evil.

Another Choleric saint, Ignatius of Loyola, did a similar about-face after he was wounded in battle and spent days reading the lives of Our Lord and the saints. He suddenly realized that he had been fighting under the wrong banner. Once his mind was made up to change, his work for God and the Church was astounding.

---

[45] Chautard, 26.

A Choleric will find virtue when he or she places their great gifts at the feet of Our Lord and asks as Paul did, "Lord, what wilt Thou have me to do?" (Acts 9:6). Our Lord had told Saul, "Arise, and go into the city, and there it shall be told thee what thou must do" (Acts 9:7). The Savior wanted him to learn to listen to others and do what he was told. Again, Saul is learning humility.

Ananias was dispatched to bring further instructions to Saul. "And the Lord said to him [Ananias]: Go thy way; for this man [Saul] is to me a vessel of election, to carry my name before the Gentiles, and kings, and the children of Israel. For I will shew him how great things he must suffer for my name's sake" (Acts 9:15–16).

Tip for Cholerics: *You will find virtue when you place your great gifts at the feet of Our Lord and ask as Paul did, "Lord, what wilt Thou have me to do?" (Acts 9:6).*

After Ananias gave him the message, the new convert spent time among the Christians of Damascus, the ones he had come this way to persecute. He humbly learned from them and prayed with them before he himself preached in the synagogue.

It takes humility and patience to ask Our Lord to show us what we must do, and then carry out His Will, not our own. Paul, Ignatius, and other great Choleric saints thus found their way to sanctity.

St. Christopher,[46] the patron saint of travelers, may well have been a Choleric too. In his story, he sought to serve the greatest king of all. As soon as he found that the king he served was afraid of someone, he looked for a greater monarch, and continued to do this until he finally found Our Lord Jesus Christ. St. Christopher could not respect someone who was

[46] Saint Christopher (third century).

frightened. Cholerics often do not understand fear since they rarely experience it. If they do experience it, sometimes it makes them angry and even more determined to accomplish their objective.

Choleric saints are notable for their great *zeal*, which comes naturally to them. If Cholerics learn to be unselfish in their ardor, then they acquire a desire to suffer for Christ. St. Francis Xavier,[47] another Choleric, is said to have became so zealous to suffer for God that he prayed, "More, O Lord, more! Take not this cross away from me unless You give me a heavier one."

St. Paul renounced the world with all its glory and kept his eyes only on Heaven. Cholerics must make the choice (as do all the temperaments) to set their sights on earthly glory or Heavenly, eternal glory. Once that choice is made with all the firmness of a Choleric's character, they will find it much easier to move toward that goal. Singleness of purpose is a natural part of the Choleric temperament.

"To enjoy completely Christ's love, was, for Paul, life itself," wrote St. John Chrysostom,[48] "the whole world, the Angels, all things present and things to come, the kingdom and the promise, since Christ's love represented for him untold blessings. He gave consideration to nothing, either pleasurable or painful, which did not point in the direction of that love."[49]

Let us be goal-oriented like St. Paul, setting our sights on eternal beatitude and the eternal love of God! If there is a Choleric in our lives who refuses to see the Truth of the Holy Roman Catholic Church, or clings to some other sin with determination, let us not give up hope. St. Paul wrote

---

[47] Saint Francis Xavier (1506–1552).

[48] Saint John Chrysostom (347–407 AD).

[49] As quoted in A Lapide, *The Personality of St. Paul*, 85.

to the Hebrews, "Let us hold fast the confession of our hope without wavering (for He is faithful that hath promised)" (Heb. 10:23). Cholerics themselves find the virtue of hope easy to master, because of their logical and strong intellects, and their natural confidence and optimism.

The same saint wrote: "Hold fast the hope set before us. Which we have as an anchor of the soul, sure and firm" (Heb. 6:18–19). Even our politicians and government leaders, when they seem hell-bent on destroying everything that a Catholic holds dear, are not outside the reach of prayer and the mercy of God.

Another virtue that comes easily to Cholerics is fortitude, or courage. Fortitude is having the strength to do God's will, despite difficulties. Choleric missionaries like Saints Paul and Francis Xavier, or great Choleric women like Saints Catherine of Siena and Teresa of Ávila, showed no fear in the undertaking of mighty adventures for Christ.

They spoke up; they spoke out; they did what God wanted them to do bravely. Therefore, He gave them great works to do in His Name. Francis Xavier went right to the Emperor of China to convert him, knowing that if he could do that, he could easily bring all of China and Japan to Christ. Paul zealously and courageously converted the mistresses of the evil Emperor Nero, the most powerful man in the world at that time. "He converted Nero's mistresses and induced them to live chastely," wrote Cornelius A Lapide, SJ, "For this reason, Paul was put to death by Nero, and became a victim of chastity, as St. John Chrysostom taught."[50] St. Gregory wrote, "Paul can be put to death, but never conquered."[51]

---

[50] A Lapide, 96.

[51] As quoted in A Lapide, 85.

St. Paul had come so far in the spiritual life and had learned so well to depend on God and not himself, that he wrote he was satisfied, for Christ's sake, in his "infirmities, in reproaches, in necessities, in persecutions, in distresses . . . For when I am weak, then am I powerful" (2 Cor. 12:10). What an amazing thing for a Choleric to say! God's grace had taken his powerful personality and turned it to zeal and fiery charity, tempered with great humility.

St. Jerome wrote: "No matter how much you humble yourself, you will never be as humble as Christ was."[52] Paul clearly took Our Lord Jesus Christ as his own model and tried heroically to imitate His humility and charity.

Paul's humility is demonstrated in his repentance. "Paul continually wept over his former disbelief and persecution of the Christians even though he had committed these sins through ignorance," wrote Cornelius A Lapide, SJ, "With deep sorrow, he often accused himself of them, and through his writings, he has transmitted the account of them to posterity down through the centuries: 'For I am the least of the Apostles, and am not worthy to be called an apostle, because I persecuted the Church of God.' (1 Cor. 15:9)."[53]

Tip for Cholerics: *Work toward humility like St. Paul, and then "go forth" to do God's Will!*

In his first letter to Timothy, St. Paul wrote: "Christ Jesus came into this world to save sinners, of whom I am the chief. But for this cause have I obtained mercy: that in me first Christ Jesus might shew forth all patience, for the information of them that shall believe in Him unto

---

52 As quoted in A Lapide, 73.

53 A Lapide, 67.

life everlasting" (1 Tim. 1:15–16). Once he realized he was wrong, Paul praised Our Lord's patience in putting up with him. He used God's patience with him as a model for how he should treat others, beseeching them to obey God's laws and to be at peace with one another.

Humility is essential for all the temperaments. The Cure d'Ars,[54] called it the string that holds the rosary of our virtues together. If we do not have humility, all the other beads of our so-called virtues will roll away and be scattered.

Tip for Cholerics: *God is patient with you, like He was with St. Paul. Use God's patience as your model for how you treat others.*

"My son, do thy works in meekness, and thou shalt be beloved above the glory of men," we read in Holy Scripture. "The greater thou art, the more humble thyself in all things, and thou shalt find grace before God: For great is the power of God alone, and He is honored by the humble" (Ecclus. 3:20–21).

Cholerics can find a model in St. Paul, acknowledging their faults and their weakness to God, and begging Him to give them strength and patience to go forth and help others. Those with this temperament have such energy; it must not go to waste. God gave them that motivation, zeal, and vigor so they might use it for His glory and the sanctification of souls.

If you are a Choleric, use your natural charisma, strength of leadership, and organizational skills to carry out the work of Almighty God. "Going therefore, teach ye all nations" (Matt. 28:19), instruct your children, be a

Tip for Cholerics: *Use your natural charisma, strength of leadership, and organizational skills to carry out the work of Almighty God.*

[54] Saint John Vianney (1786–1859).

good example to your friends, and pursue the mission you have been given in the Almighty's plan.

But first you may have to *find* that mission, like our next saint: Teresa of Ávila.

3

St. Teresa Finds Her Mission

Choleric-Sanguine

Saint Teresa of Ávila was born on March 28, 1515, in the beautiful walled city of Ávila, Spain. She was baptized on April 4, the same day that the Carmelite Convent of the Incarnation opened in her city. Her father had a son Juan and a daughter Maria from his first marriage. When his wife died, he remarried. He and his second wife, Dona Beatriz, had Fernando, Rodrigo, Teresa, Lorenzo, Antonio, Pedro, Jeronimo, and Juana. Teresa had one much older sister, one much younger sister, and seven brothers.

Teresa's mother died when she was thirteen years old. In 1531, her older sister Maria married, leaving Teresa the oldest daughter and head of her father's household at only sixteen years old. Beautiful, rich, and born of a noble house, she became flirtatious and worldly but never fell into serious sin. She read stories of chivalry and romance, which of course were not as filthy as some of today's romance novels, and had her share of crushes on the handsome, rich young men with whom she came in contact. These interests and tendencies show us the Sanguine side of her temperament.

Her serious father became concerned over her behavior and sent her to boarding school at the convent of Our Lady of Grace, run by Augustinian nuns. Teresa was not happy to miss out on all the partying, but her biographer, Auclair, tells us that, "her new companions loved her, for God had given her the gift of pleasing people wherever she went."[55] She learned to pray and turn more toward God, and eventually felt the call to the religious life.

Strangely, her father would not let her enter the convent. But Teresa was a strong-willed Choleric. "When I want something, I want it for all I'm worth," she declared.[56] When she was eighteen, she ran away to be a nun. When her father came to get her, she persuaded him that she was right, and he not only gave his permission, but provided her a dowry. As we learn about her life and personality, this decisiveness, mixed with lawyer-like persuasiveness, shows us her nature.

The Convent of the Incarnation at Ávila used the "mitigated" Carmelite rule, which was quite lax. The nuns had large rooms with their own kitchens and invited their lay friends over for meals and chatting. After twenty-seven years as a nun at the Incarnation, Teresa felt called to open a convent of the old rule. Amid many contradictions, she proceeded to travel up and down Spain, opening sixteen convents for women and working with St. John of the Cross[57] to found the same kind of order for men. These reformed convents became the birthplaces of sanctity for many.

---

[55] Auclair, *Saint Teresa of Avila*, 25.
[56] As quoted in Auclair, 41.
[57] Saint John of the Cross (1542–1591).

She wrote *The Way of Perfection*, *The Interior Castle*, and her autobiography, all of which are read and studied today for inspiration and wisdom. Teresa died on October 4, 1582, at the age of sixty-seven. She is buried at Alba de Tormes, not far from Ávila, and her body is incorrupt.

Cholerics make the best catechists and apostles, whether they are physically present, like St. Paul, or from behind a cloistered convent's walls, like St. Teresa. "A single burning prayer of the seraphic St. Teresa (as was learned through a highly creditable revelation) converted ten thousand heretics," wrote Dom Chautard in *The Soul of the Apostolate*, "And her soul, all on fire for Christ, could not conceive of a contemplative life, an interior life, which would take no interest in the Savior's intense anxiety for the redemption of souls."[58]

St. Teresa's name is synonymous with proficiency and expertise in prayer. She believed in its efficacy for every soul, without exception. She wrote unswervingly, "Take my advice and let no one mislead you by pointing out any other way than prayer. I am not discussing here whether mental and vocal prayer are necessary for everybody; but I contend that you require both."[59] Peter Rohrbach's excellent book on the teachings of St. Teresa on personal prayer, *Conversation with Christ*, breaks down her sixteenth-century writings on prayer for a modern audience.

Mental prayer was her anchor as well as her weapon. Marcelle Auclair, in her dynamic biography of Teresa, wrote,

[58] Chautard, *Soul of the Apostolate*, 37.

[59] Teresa of Ávila, *Way of Perfection*, xxi; as cited in Rohrbach, *Conversation with Christ*, 8.

"Prayer can be warfare, silence a fortress, and mortification, strategy; a soul centered in God is as mighty as armies on the march, and women who are silent and still under their black veil can fight for the peace of the world by making every single thought, every single sacrifice 'an heroic act.'"[60]

Cholerics, as we saw in the life of St. Paul, love to "go forth" and conquer new lands, whether by starting a ground-breaking computer company or by going to the New World to spread the Gospel. The Choleric St. Ignatius courageously founded the Jesuit Order to be a special army that answered only to the pope. St. Teresa herself discovered a new frontier. "In her search for adventure," writes Auclair, "She had discovered a limitless world, vaster and richer than any land beyond the seas and one more difficult to conquer: her interior self."[61]

Tip for Cholerics: *Explore the wild frontier of your own soul—learn to conquer it for Christ!*

People with a Choleric temperament do not fear hard work if they feel it is important. They despise laziness and can become workaholics. They are also eminently practical. They see what must be done and move forward to accomplish it. St. Teresa turned her efforts inward and explored the relationship between God and the human soul. In 1577, at the age of sixty-two, she completed her spiritual classic: *The Interior Castle,* or *The Seven Mansions of the Soul.*

Attaining concentrated prayer and true self-knowledge is hard work. They require consistent digging, control of one's thoughts, and deep humility. St. Teresa admits that it was often hard for her to work through distractions and

---

[60] Auclair, *Saint Teresa of Avila*, 170.

[61] Auclair, 28.

temptations, even after years of mental prayer. But she offers these words of encouragement and hope in her book, *Way of Perfection*, "Besides the courage we ought to have in the combat of mental prayer, we must also be firmly convinced that, unless we allow ourselves to be vanquished, our efforts will be crowned with success."[62] We cannot lose this battle unless we surrender. As long as we keep fighting, "our efforts will be crowned with success."

St. Teresa's *Determinacion*

We talked about the firm resolve of St. Paul and how St. Francis de Sales made a decided resolution to become a saint. Auclair writes that the keyword of St. Teresa's life, as we mentioned previously, was *determinacion*. She quotes the saint, "All is already as good as done when a soul *determines* to practice mental prayer," and, "Those who have this determination have nothing to fear."[63]

When we make solid resolutions to find the will of God in all things and perform it wholeheartedly, God gives us the merits of those actions even if we are prevented from their completion. He sees the heart; He sees our intention. Therefore, our intention should always be pure: "Whatsoever you do, do it from the heart, as to the Lord, and not to men" (Col. 3:23).

St. Alphonsus tells us, "Without prayer we have no communication with God, which would enable us to preserve

---

[62] Teresa of Avila, *Way of Perfection*, xxiii; as quoted in Rohrbach, *Conversation with Christ*, 27.

[63] As quoted in Auclair, *Saint Teresa of Avila*, 36.

virtue. Without prayer, we have an imperfect knowledge of the wants of our soul, the dangers to which our salvation is exposed, or the means to overcome temptations."[64] Once we have the desired intentions, prayer helps us align our actions to the will of God.

Saint Teresa spent her apostolate encouraging prayer, teaching others to pray, and showing the importance of both mental prayer (meditation) and vocal prayer (praying aloud either alone or with others). A classic anecdote tells us that one day, Our Lord said to her, "I would speak to many souls, but the world makes such a noise in their ears, that I would not be heard." She knew the power of silent prayer and tried to share this good news with everyone with whom she came in contact.

Saint Teresa also had a healthy dose of Sanguine in her temperament. Sanguines want very much to be loved. Their tendency to be "people pleasers" can lead to their downfall. Saint Teresa, as a Choleric-Sanguine combination, longed to be loved. She found that desired satisfaction in her profound relationship with God in the depths of her soul.

She battled through incredible hardships when she knew it was God's will. Though Sanguines can become discouraged if he or she feels resistance from others, it is hard to discourage a Choleric when his or her mind is set on something.

"Teresa did become a saint by sheer force of willing it and with the grace of God," wrote Auclair. "It is this process of achieving sanctity, the slow and costly transformation, that makes her life an unparalleled example for us."[65]

---

[64] de Ligouri, *The Love of Our Lord*, 82.

[65] Auclair, *Saint Teresa of Avila*, 44.

As a child, she was already showing her Choleric temperament. She and her brother read about the lives of the martyrs and decided to join them. For a Choleric, decisions come easily, and action even more easily. So off they went, two little kids, to find their way to Africa so they could be martyred by the Muslims. Brave? Yes! Decisive? Yes! Resourceful? Yes! But not exactly prudent. Fortunately, an uncle met them on their way out of the city and hustled them home.

Tip for Parents of Choleric Children: *Do not crush their spirit. Instead, direct that willfulness and spirit into more prudent channels of virtue.*

It is never good to crush the spirit of a Choleric child. Little Teresa's idea was admirable but misguided. It is better to direct that willfulness and spirit into more prudent channels of virtue. Her Choleric personality showed again when she played convent with her cousins. Auclair writes, "Dressed up as a little nun, she obliged her cousins to the observance of a rule drawn up by herself. Naturally she was prioress."[66]

St. Teresa's Union with Christ in the Eucharist

In addition to St. Teresa's *determinacion* and devotion to prayer, there was another powerful aid that helped her grow in holiness: her union with Christ in the Holy Eucharist.

Father Louis Lallemant, SJ referred to an invaluable way of overcoming our faults and growing in virtue: the frequent reception of Holy Communion. He wrote, "Our Lord, uniting His Body to our body and His Soul to our soul,

[66] Auclair, 11.

burns and consumes within us the seeds of our own vices, and communicates to us by degrees His own divine temperament and perfections, according as we are disposed and suffer Him to operate in us."[67]

Father Lallemant goes on to say that, with frequent Communion, Our Lord can help us with the little (and big) irritations in our lives that become a "seed of vexation." He says that Our Lord "effaces the remembrance and image of this discontent; he obliterates the impression which has been left on all our powers, and entirely destroys that seed of sins, putting in its place the fruits of charity, joy, peace, and patience. He tears up in like manner the roots of anger, intemperance, and our other faults, and communicates to us the virtues and their fruits."[68]

> ***Tip for all Temperaments:*** *Receive Our Lord in Holy Communion, fervently and frequently.*

The more often we receive Our Lord in Holy Communion, the more we become like Him. Just as the Host dissolves and literally becomes a part of us when we consume It, our souls become one with Jesus Christ. We know that St. Teresa treasured her times of communion with Christ in the Eucharist. St. John of the Cross is thought to have described her times of communion as such: "At times rays of light and splendor seemed to come from her eyes and forehead, filling those who watched her with awe. . . . When receiving Holy Communion, and even before she had swallowed the sacred Host, her face became extraordinarily beautiful and transparent. She looked so majestic and grave that I felt the

---

[67] Lallemant, *Spiritual Doctrine*, 167.

[68] Lallemant, 167.

deepest reverence for her, it was easy to see Who was her Guest, and how she had received Him."[69]

Everyone, regardless of temperament, will benefit from frequent, fervent reception of Holy Communion. In addition to being in the state of sanctifying grace and making a Communion fast before we receive Him, St. Alphonsus tells us that we should also have an insatiable desire to love Our Lord more and more. If we receive Him out of love, and to increase our love, we cannot fail to grow spiritually.

The Choleric side of St. Teresa knew something Good—something Infinitely Good—could be found in the Eucharist, and she pursued It with *determinacion*. The Sanguine side of St. Teresa wanted to give and receive love, and she found that in the sweetness of Holy Communion.

As St. Teresa approached the end of her life, she asked for her last Communion—Holy Viaticum. Her reception of Holy Viaticum is relayed as follows:

> The Sisters wept and prayed in silence until they heard the tinkling of the bell which announced that the priest was bringing the Blessed Sacrament. Although for the last two days, the help of two nuns had been required to lift the holy Mother in bed, she now rose quickly of her own accord and knelt upon the mattress. So strong was the impulse of her love . . . that, had she not been prevented, she would have cast herself upon the ground to receive her Master. Her face was majestic and beautiful, and looked far younger than her real age.

---

[69] *Minor Works of St. Teresa*, 223. The Benedictines attribute this quote to St. John of the Cross, who knew and worked with St. Teresa.

> With clasped hands and soul aflame with love, her face illumined with joy, she began . . . as her life was ebbing away, a song far sweeter than any she had sung before. "O my Bridegroom, my Master!" she exclaimed, "at last the longed-for hour has come! Now it is time for us to see one another! My Master, it is time to set forth! Blessed be this hour, and may Thy Will be done! Now is the hour for me to leave this desert that my soul may rejoice in Thee Whom it has so ardently desired." She would have continued her colloquy much longer, had not her superior bidden her under obedience to be silent, lest she should harm herself.[70]

What love, what consolation, she received from the Holy Eucharist throughout her life, and at the end of it!

Cholerics, because of their direct thinking, are often outspoken. Teresa of Ávila, with her great love for Our Lord, and her great prayer life and active life, often spoke her mind. In 1582, she was traveling through terrible floods to open another Carmelite convent, this time in Burgos, Spain. There had been no bed for them at the inn, the bridges had been washed away by the floods, and now she was trying to cross the raging River Arlanzon, with carriages full of nuns.

"Those who were on the bank," wrote Marcelle Auclair, "saw her carriage swerve and stop as it hung over the torrent: the Foundress jumped out into water which came halfway up her legs, she was not very agile and hurt herself. As always,

---

70 *Minor Works of St. Teresa*, 211–212; quoting from Fuentes, *Obras*, l.c., 223.

her cry was a calling upon God: this time she complained: 'Lord, amid so many ills this comes on top of all the rest!' The Voice answered her: 'Teresa, that is how I treat My friends.'"[71]

Tip for Sanguines: *Use your natural charm to bring people to God and the path of virtue.*

The forthright saint responded, "Ah my God! That is why You have so few of them!" She did not mean to be disrespectful or not insubmissive to God's will. As a devoted nun, Our Lord was her Divine Spouse, and she was merely reproaching Him lovingly. In modern-day language, she probably would have said, "I say it like it is!"

Cholerics sometimes use their wit as a weapon. Saint Teresa of Ávila prayed, "From silly devotions, and from sour-faced saints, good Lord deliver us!"[72] But if they are balanced, they can turn their wit on themselves for the amusement of others. She wrote books on the spiritual life, including her own autobiography, but she also wrote self-deprecatingly, "So many books have been written by learned and holy men that there is nothing left for a woman to write about!"[73]

Let us consider her Sanguine side. She was captivating, and she was "kind and merry."[74] Choleric-Sanguines are good at getting what they want, because they have tenacity and focus mixed with charm and people skills. God can do a lot with Choleric-Sanguines if they place themselves in His Hands.

Auclair writes that "her charm was irresistible," and mentions "her lively and continually changing expression,"[75] which

---

[71] Auclair, *Saint Teresa of Avila*, 391.

[72] Roche, *A Bedside Book of Saints*, 69–70.

[73] Roche, 70.

[74] Auclair, *Saint Teresa of Avila*, 14.

[75] Auclair, 15.

is another indication that she was part Sanguine. The faces of Sanguines are very mobile, and their moods can change quickly.

Fray Luis de Leon, as quoted by Auclair, writes, "Her beauty and the care she took of her person, her polished conversation, the sweetness and refinement of her manners made her more attractive still. Saint and sinner, ascetic and worldling, old and young alike came under the influence of her charm, though this in no way detracted from her dignity. Child or growing girl, in the world or as a nun, she attracted all who came in contact with her as the magnet draws steel."[76]

When her father sent her to a convent school, the Sisters were able to direct and help her. She was guided by a nun who understood her nature: Sister Maria de Briceno, a thirty-six-year-old noblewoman. Auclair describes St. Teresa at this stage of life as "impressionable . . . so impulsive and ready to translate words into action that a mere spark of feeling would kindle the fire needed to bring a project to immediate realization . . . her actions had always been prompted by enthusiasm."[77] This excitement and optimism, joined with impulsive decisiveness and follow-through, define someone who is Sanguine and Choleric. Such a person can come up with a great idea, sell it to those around him or her, and follow through with it; Saint Teresa had these qualities.

When she was eighteen, she ran away to be a nun, because she asked her father, and he refused to give his permission. This St. Teresa was so different from the Little Flower, St. Thérèse,[78] who also was forbidden the permission to become a

---

[76] Auclair, 15.

[77] Auclair, 27.

[78] Saint Thérèse of Lisieux (1873–1897).

religious but obeyed her father and waited to enter. St. Thérèse was Melancholic, and St. Teresa was Choleric and Sanguine.

Saint Teresa considered herself inconsistent, because of the mixture of Choleric and Sanguine in her personality. Within the following quote, let us note in brackets the Choleric and Sanguine attributes. Auclair says, "She was proud [Choleric], but frivolous [Sanguine]: domineering [Choleric], but easily influenced [Sanguine], she talks of herself as being 'terribly given to subterfuge' [Sanguine] and yet mentions her horror of lies [Choleric, and her spiritual training], or again of her liking to please people [Sanguine] which does not, however, bridle a quick temper liable to break out into 'terrible' rages [Choleric]."[79]

She loved to talk a lot, wear bright colors, and be the center of attention, all very Sanguine characteristics. But as a novice, she worked diligently to become quieter and more reserved. She applied her Choleric strength of will to the silliness (a weakness of the Sanguine), and thereby managed to become less shallow and more productive, while keeping the personability and charm of the Sanguine. An old book on the life of this saint alludes to the fact that she was like "silk of a golden color which matches every other shade"[80] because she would adapt her methods to the person with whom she was dealing. She would laugh with the Sanguines, discuss battle plans with the Cholerics, sympathize with the Melancholics, and speak quietly with the Phlegmatics. Sanguines often have this gift of adjusting to others, and thereby find a connection with each person.

---

[79] Auclair, *Saint Teresa of Avila*, 44.

[80] As quoted in Auclair, 50.

People sometimes laughingly ask why handsome men are called to be priests. It could be that God is using their natural attractiveness to draw people to listen to them. Someone who is pretty or handsome, and who speaks well and charmingly, is more likely to be heard than someone who is disagreeable in appearance and speech. People who knew St. Teresa in life referred to her as attractive and charming.

She liked to use the imagery of castles, chivalric conquests, and battles. If we were able to talk to her about the temperaments, she would have seen the wisdom of evaluating our arsenal before entering the combat of self-conquest. What are my strengths? What are my weapons? What are my weaknesses? What are the chinks in my armor?

Tip for Sanguines: *You have a gift for connecting with many different types of people. Use your charismatic appeal for God's work.*

When she first became a novice, "She did not know how to use the Breviary or how to behave in choir," writes David Lewis, MA, one of her biographers. "She knew the other novices could have taught her, but 'I never asked them,' she says, 'that they might not know how little I knew.'"[81] Cholerics never want to show ignorance or weakness. They will confidently march down the street, discover that it is the wrong way, and confidently march back the other way with an attitude that says, "I meant to do that!"

Saint Teresa had been the best at everything when she was in the world. She did not relish the discovery that she was not the holiest and most proficient nun at the Convent of the Incarnation. She admitted in her autobiography, according to Auclair, "My singing was bad . . . Finally I forced myself

[81] As quoted in Lewis, *Saint Teresa*, 5.

to say so when I didn't know how something went. This cost me a good deal at the beginning but afterwards I found pleasure in it."[82] Cholerics in particular can learn from this. Do you hesitate to ask for help because you do not want anyone to know your ignorance? Instead, force yourself to ask for help, and it will become easier, like it did for St. Teresa. It will also help us to acquire the virtue of humility.

Tip for Cholerics and Sanguines: *Admit when you need guidance or instruction, even if it is humbling to do so.*

When Our Lord wishes to raise a Choleric to great heights of sanctity, He often humbles the person first, into the very dust, like St. Paul. For Saint Teresa, she became terribly sick, so that she was paralyzed for three years. When, through the intercession of St. Joseph, she regained her health, she endured a rough patch, in which people believed that her meditations and visions were from the devil. Our Lord "prepared her and directed her Himself through the furnace of that which was in reality the persecution or contradiction of good men, which is one of the greatest trials of saints."[83]

Although Cholerics do not shy away from confrontation (many enjoy the challenge), when a Choleric is pursuing the path of sanctity, he deeply hurt when devout people persecute him. This is what happened to so many of the saints, of all different temperaments. We should not be surprised when it happens nowadays because, "It is one of the greatest trials of saints."

Saint Teresa learned humility by these many humiliations. During her time of sickness, she learned to reach great

[82] As quoted in Auclair, *Saint Teresa of Avila*, 47.
[83] Lewis, *Saint Teresa*, 14.

heights of mental prayer. In her day, convents had become very social, lax places. She would never have had all that time for prayer if she had been socializing in the convent parlor every day, sipping sangria with her friends. She also learned the hard lesson of obedience, because she did the right thing when she was criticized: she subjected all her visions, ideas, and ecstasies to a good spiritual director. Sometimes, she was asked to recount the state of her soul and her spiritual graces and gifts to numerous spiritual experts, and she learned to do this in humility. In doing so, some consoled her, while others persecuted her. Through these huge trials, she learned to trust God, and not herself.

After Our Lord humbles Choleric, like Saints Teresa of Ávila or Paul of Tarsus, with great trials and tribulations, He then builds them back up again on a foundation of humility and confidence in God. In this second phase of their lives, He uses their strength of character, decisive determination, and energy to serve *Him*, instead of the world and themselves. Saint Francis Xavier and Saint Catherine of Siena had similar experiences and accomplished breathtaking things for the glory of God and the salvation of souls.

With her Choleric will and her Sanguine charm, she was one of the most influential women of her time. Next, we will take a look at a saint with an even stronger Sanguine tendency—Simon, who became Peter.

4

Simon is "Petrified"

Sanguine

Saint Peter, formerly known as Simon Bar-Jona (son of Jona), was born about the year AD 1, in Bethsaida. He lived in Capernaum, and archaeologists believe they have unearthed his house there. He made his living by fishing with his brother, Andrew, on the Sea of Galilee.

Through St. John the Baptist, Andrew found Our Lord and learned that He was the Messiah. As faithful Jews, Simon and Andrew had anticipated and prayed for His coming. Andrew excitedly shared the news with his brother and introduced him to Our Lord.

Jesus said, "Thou art Simon the son of Jona: thou shalt be called Cephas, which is interpreted Peter" (Jn. 1:42). The three years that Peter spent following Our Lord—and his abandonment of the Savior when He was arrested, beaten, and crucified—are laid out for us in Holy Scripture.

We continue to read of the repentant Peter in the Acts of the Apostles. After the descent of the Holy Ghost upon the apostles, Peter's preaching converted thousands. He ruled over the infant Church as its first pope, fulfilling Christ's prophecy, "Thou art Peter; and upon this rock I will build

My Church" (Matt. 16:18). Peter traveled a good deal (though not as much as Paul) and finally went to Rome, the center of civilization at that time. Around the year AD 67, he was martyred for his Catholic Faith by crucifixion in Rome, on Vatican Hill, where St. Peter's Basilica now stands.

Anyone who knows a Sanguine would hardly call them "steady as a rock." Yet the omniscient and infallible Master looked at Sanguine Simon with love in His eyes and said, "Thou art Peter; and upon this rock I will build My Church" (Matt. 16:18). We describe wood that has hardened like stone as petrified, from the Latin word *petra*, meaning "rock." Our Lord changed Simon's name literally to "The Rock."

Peter was full of faith and full of courage. Who else but a Sanguine would ask Our Lord to prove His identity and His divinity by letting a mere Galilean fisherman walk on the water toward Him? "And they seeing Him walk upon the sea, were troubled, saying: It is an apparition. And they cried out for fear. And immediately Jesus spoke to them, saying: Be of good heart: it is I, fear ye not. And Peter making answer, said: Lord, if it be Thou, bid me come to Thee upon the waters. And He said: Come" (Matt. 14:26–29).

Did Our Lord smile to Himself when He said, "Come"? We cannot imagine any of the other apostles asking, "Is it really You, Lord, walking on the water when the wind is so 'contrary'? And if it is, can I walk on the water, too?" Such faith! Such eagerness and such

Tip for Sanguines: *Use your natural impetuosity to jump into doing things for God, and not leap into endeavors unworthy of your abilities.*

a desire to do something fun! But when Peter gets out of the boat and takes a few steps, being Sanguine, his mood changes! Suddenly, he is terrified to find himself walking on the water in the middle of a strong wind.

If you are Sanguine, learn from Peter's fear, and from Our Lord's gentle rebuke about keeping faith. Anchor your faith and hope in Him Who walks on water, and not in your own strength. Peter slipped and almost drowned when he took his eyes off Jesus and looked down at himself, walking on the water.

Later in Scripture, Peter showed his great faith again when Our Lord asked, "Whom do you say that I am?" (Matt. 16:15).

"Simon Peter answered and said: Thou art Christ, the Son of the living God" (Matt. 16:16). Our Lord blessed Peter and told him that He would give him the keys of the kingdom of Heaven. What a reward for his faith! Our Lord *knew* Peter would deny Him and leave Him during His passion, but still, He generously recompensed Peter's profession of faith. He foresaw Peter's weakness and betrayal in His omniscient wisdom, and yet He said, "Thou art Peter; and upon this rock I will build My Church, and the gates of hell shall not prevail against it" (Matt. 16:18). God knew that this passionate Sanguine, from a hardworking family by the sea of Galilee, had the potential to be a rock for the foundation of the entire Catholic Church. What hope this gives to Sanguines!

We are moved when we read the part in Scripture where Our Lord asks sadly of His followers, "And will you also leave Me?" (see Jn. 6:68) because so many disciples abandoned Him. They had been scandalized and confused when He taught the doctrine of the Eucharist, and Our Lord was saddened to see His message of love rejected. Peter is the hero of this scene. He exclaims, "Lord, to whom shall we go? Thou hast the words of eternal life" (Jn. 6:69). Peter's exclamation must have warmed Our Lord's heart.

The Master, knowing the intricacies of the human heart, keeps encouraging Peter, giving him opportunities to protest his faith and love and coaxing him along in the spiritual life. When the Lord moved toward Peter to wash his feet at the Last Supper, Peter protested, but Our Lord cleverly told him, "If I wash thee not, thou shalt have no part with me" (Jn. 13:8). Our Lord was the quintessential psychologist; He knew how Peter would respond. Peter immediately exclaimed, "Lord, not only my feet, but also my hands and my head!" (Jn. 13:9). Once the Sanguine understands the situation, then he or she wants to throw themselves in, heart and soul. His enthusiasm was admirable, but Peter, like all Sanguines, had to work on his lack of consistency. Our Lord helped him, step by step, just as He helps us.

Tip for Parents of Sanguine Children: *Keep giving them encouragement, and help them, step by step, to learn consistency.*

"[Peter] is all impulse and impetuosity," writes Father A. Galy, SM, "His ardent love is bubbling over at every moment. He is restless, agitated; he has no peace whenever there is question of the Master."[84] Peter, in his Sanguine optimism, also believes in his own loyalty to the Savior, and does not think he could possibly let Him down. This is where he must learn humility. Sanguines need just as much humility as Cholerics.

In the Garden of Gethsemane, Peter may have fallen asleep with the others while Our Lord suffered His agony, but St. John

[84] Galy, *The Friend of Sinners*, 154.

tells us that he leaped up with his sword in his hand to defend Our Lord when He was endangered by the Pharisees and their soldiers. Quietly praying at night in a dark garden after a full meal was not easy for Peter. Our Lord's warnings of His departure troubled him, and he was a man of action. When action was needed, either to jump overboard and swim to shore, or draw his sword and cut off the ear of the man threatening Jesus's safety, Peter's love and courage never wavered.

Our Lord gently rebuked Peter in the garden, however, and told him that this was not the time for the sword. He healed the ear of Malchus, the servant of the High Priest, and left Peter scared and baffled. Peter, like other Jews of his time, believed that Our Lord was going to restore the earthly kingdom of Israel. How could He do that if He were bound in chains and led away under the power of His enemies? When Our Lord would not let Peter physically defend Him, Peter did not understand. This was a time of great trial for him.

> ***Tips for Sanguines and Cholerics:***
> *In times of enforced inaction, cultivate patience. God's timing is perfect.*

Our Lord had been trying to teach him the lesson of self-sacrifice. He had told Peter, as we read in the Gospel of Matthew, to forgive his brother seventy times seven times (see Matt. 18:22). Jesus had advised him that if someone steals his cloak, Peter should run after him and give him his coat too (see Matt. 5:40). But Peter had not grasped this concept completely yet. When Our Lord was led away meekly in chains, Peter did not know what to do. In fear, discouragement, and ignorance, he ran away from Gethsemane. But Peter's love had not died, and he stealthily pursued Our

Lord, going to the palace of Caiphas to learn the fate of the Lord he loved and followed.

Peter's self-confidence was shaken when Our Lord told him to put his sword away, but he did not place his trust in God. He continued to rely on his own strength, a mistake we all make at one time or another. God is all-powerful; we are weak. Leaning on his own strength, Peter denies Our Lord three times when he is asked if he knows the Savior. How humiliating! Like the Choleric Paul, the Sanguine Peter had to learn humility by his own fall.

Tip for Sanguines: *Have faith, but anchor that faith in God and not yourself, for you, like all of us, are weak and changeable.*

As Our Lord is being taken away, He passes by Peter. Saint Luke, in a masterful understatement, writes simply, "And the Lord turning looked on Peter" (Luke 22:61). We can only imagine the depth of that look: such profound sorrow, unspeakable kindness, and gentle and kindly reproach. This glance converted Peter. The look in Our Lord's eyes gave Peter the "good sadness" that St. Francis de Sales tells us about in his writings on the spiritual life.

Usually, sadness is no good to us and only makes life harder (see chapter 9). But there is a rare, special sadness, like the one that pierced the heart of Peter in that moment. "For the sorrow that is according to God worketh penance, steadfast unto salvation; but the sorrow of the world worketh death," wrote St. Paul, years later. (2 Cor. 7:10).

The good kind of sadness brought tranquility and peace to Peter. He realized he was weak, and that he had done wrong, but he also knew Our Lord's forgiveness was available to him. He wept copiously with tears of true repentance. His tears did not spring from self-pity nor from thinking, "How could this have happened to me, when I was going to be so brave?" Instead, he wept for the sorrow he had caused to the Master whom he loved.

"Good sadness gives strength and courage and does not allow us to leave off or abandon a good design," wrote St. Francis de Sales.[85] "Good sadness opens the mind, makes it serene and luminous . . . gives understanding . . . proceeding from God, [it] increases our confidence in Him, and makes us pray and invoke His mercy."[86] That is how we know whether it is good or bad sadness. We must discern the difference, so we are not depressed and discouraged by the devil's version of sadness, the one that makes us give up trying to grow closer to God.

Tip for Sanguines: *Beware of the harmful sadness that discourages us from spiritual growth.*

Through this beautiful penitence following Our Lord's glance of reproach and love, Peter found his way to anchoring his faith and his impulses in God, and not himself. He threw his grappling hook into the cliff-face of God's own majestic strength and steadfastness, and there found his strength.

"Peter now loves with true and complete affection and because he is naturally of so active a temperament, his love will be active and the activity will be immense," wrote Fr. Galy. "Humility becomes one of his constant traits, and shielded by this virtue, his love will become invincible."[87]

---

[85] de Sales, *Consoling Thoughts on Trials of an Interior Life*, 95.

[86] de Sales, 95.

[87] Galy, *The Friend of Sinners*, 160.

After talking about the repentance of St. Paul in his book, *The Personality of St. Paul*, Cornelius A Lapide, SJ wrote, "St. Peter, too, at the crowing of the cock every dawn, fell upon his knees, and weeping profusely for having denied Christ, asked for pardon. His eyes became inflamed and bloodshot and, on his cheeks, appeared two furrows, as if grooved by abundant tears. St. Clement, an eyewitness and disciple of St. Peter, testified to this fact and Niceforus reported it."[88] He never forgot the lesson he had learned about his own weakness. In his daily life, he may have still slipped up occasionally, but he never denied his Master again.

Sometimes Sanguines have to pick themselves up repeatedly and try again, because they have a tendency to weakness and inconsistency. St. Philip Neri was a great spiritual director of souls. One story about St. Philip Neri describes how he helped a young man who kept falling into the same serious sin over and over, even though he was trying to beat it. St. Philip Neri told him, "Every time you fall into this sin, come to Confession and I will absolve you." The young man protested that, despite his best efforts, he fell every day. The saint told him to come every day then. After several days of coming to repent, the young man found the strength to resist temptation, and finally overcame his bad habit.

> ***Tip for Sanguines:***
> *Even if you have fallen a moment ago, repent, profess your love, and move forward.*

Our dear Lord knew that Peter had repented wholeheartedly, and when He rose from the dead three days later, He wished to encourage him and let him know that he was forgiven. So, He sent him a special message. "Go, tell His

[88] A Lapide, *Personality of St. Paul*, 67–68.

disciples and Peter that He goeth before you into Galilee;" the angel told the holy women. "There you shall see Him, as He told you" (Mark 16:7).

Our Lord so easily could have left "and Peter" out of the message, but He wanted Peter to know he was forgiven and that the Lord wanted to see him again. Peter could easily have said that he no longer deserved to be called a disciple, but Jesus included him by name.

He even gave Peter the chance three times to profess his love, as a penance for his threefold denial. The Lord asked Peter, "lovest thou Me?" (Jn. 21:15). Peter did not realize what Our Lord was doing, and as He asked for the third time, Peter said piteously, "Lord, Thou knowest all things: Thou *knowest* that I love Thee!" (Jn. 21:17, emphasis added.)

Naturally, God knew that Peter loved Him; He just wanted the poor fisherman to profess it and act upon it. That is all He wants any of us to do: profess our faith and love, and act on it.

Caryll Houselander asks, "Who but Christ would have known that the one thing that could lift up that broken heart was not a formal act of contrition, but a spontaneous, almost an exasperated cry of love:? who but He would have thought of provoking the same impulsive temperament which had made a coward of Peter with such cruel results, to give it the courage to break out into those acts of love?"[89]

God wanted Peter to use that impulsive love, that warm effervescence of charity, to become the leader of the infant Catholic Church. He wanted him to use that fatherly love to become a shepherd to all the sheep in Christ's fold. Rather

---

[89] Houselander, *The Risen Christ*, 43.

than crushing Peter's spirit and temperament, He uplifted it, as He does to all of us.

"[Peter's] first sermon converts three thousand of his hearers; his second sermon, five thousand!" points out Fr. Galy.[90] Truly, Peter had hit his stride, no longer waffling back and forth, claiming he would die for the Lord one moment, and denying Him the next. He found his strength in the Lord and used his natural gifts to bring souls to God. Imagine how engaging his sermons probably became. God's grace perfected the work that He began in Peter when He created him a storytelling, laughing, optimistic, encouraging, and cheerful Sanguine.

"Wherein you shall greatly rejoice," Peter wrote in his first Epistle, "If now you must be for a little time made sorrowful in divers temptations: That the trial of your faith (much more precious than gold which is tried by the fire) may be found unto praise and glory and honor at the appearing of Jesus Christ: Whom having not seen, you love: in Whom also now, though you see Him not, you believe: and believing shall rejoice with joy unspeakable and glorified!" (1 Ptr. 1:6–8). We see how encouraging and joyful he is, and how he directs that cheerful optimism into helping others find the joy that will never end.

> ***Tip for Sanguines:***
> *Pin your joyous hopes on God and share your heavenly optimism with others.*

King Herod threw Peter in prison, after having killed James, the brother of John. Peter had every reason to believe that he would be martyred too, but he had learned the secret of inner peace. His confidence was in God and not in his

[90] Galy, *The Friend of Sinners*, 160.

own courage. All the Christians were beseeching God for his safety, but he rested in the confidence that God would take care of him.

Scripture tells us that four files of soldiers were watching him, and that he spent the night between two soldiers, chained to them. If we were chained to two soldiers in a prison, with four files of soldiers outside guarding it, and we knew that our friend James had just been killed, we might understandably be a little nervous. Hopefully, we would be praying for courage and strength, and we would be trusting in God, but we would not be sleeping soundly like Peter.

Peter slept so heavily that when an angel of the Lord came and filled the prison with light, he did not stir. "And he striking Peter on the side, raised him up, saying: Arise quickly" (Acts 12:7). In the next verse, we learn that the angel hit him on the side and ordered, "Wake up and get dressed!" The chains fell from Peter's hands, and he, rather dazedly (and perhaps sleepily) followed the angel outside the prison walls. When the angel disappeared, he realized that he had been delivered from the hand of Herod by a miracle. He then peacefully made his way to where he knew the Christians would be gathered and praying for him. They were incredulous too, telling the girl who answered the door that she must be mad to think it was Peter. What a rock Peter had become! He told the Christians to be at peace and calmly told them about the miracle.

Sanguines, who find joy in the little things of life as well as the big, can help all of us to serve the Lord more joyfully and lightheartedly. "The Saints knew that efforts, to be permanent, must be joyful efforts," wrote Father Aloysius Roche, "that without great courage and an unshaken confidence, we shall find it very difficult to persevere."[91] St. Peter learned to unite his joyful efforts to great courage and confidence in God.

One of the weaknesses of Sanguines is that they often turn to the world for the enjoyment, satisfaction, and attention that God alone can give. A clear conscience offers us a peace that the world cannot give, but very often, a Sanguine dawdles along the route of temptation, flirting with immodesty, watching a movie that "isn't really that bad; they don't *show* anything," dating a man or woman who's very worldly, saying that "she's got a good heart" or "all he needs is the influence of a good woman." The Sanguine is left with a slightly besmirched conscience and uneasiness because, although they do not *think* they have fallen into mortal sin, they are not quite as innocent as they were before. This is because the Sanguine wants so much to have fun and receive attention and applause. Even St. Teresa of Ávila, as we mentioned in the last section, was prone to worldliness and vanity because of her Sanguine nature.

In times of hurt, fear, or confusion, it is easy to turn to the world and its habitual comforts. A Choleric may reach inside to find strength, striving for control and mastery over those around them instead of turning to God, but a Sanguine turns to the world, to others, to fill his or her emotional needs. Instead, we all need to turn to God to fill us up, to satisfy our needs and our desires. Even those worldly things that are not sinful are unable to give us what our dear Master can.

Sanguines often have difficulty differentiating between pleasure and happiness. Pleasure comes from temporal

---

91 Roche, *A Bedside Book of Saints*, 46–47.

worldly delights and is usually fleeting. It is associated with our senses. Even when not sinful, pleasure does not offer us deep and lasting peace, but at best, a temporary distraction. We are not meant to be fulfilled by these pleasures. A good meal, a glass of wine, a sunset, a symphony, a stroll through a fragrant garden: these are sensual pleasures and are innocent in and of themselves. They can lift us up when the devil tries to give us the rotten kind of sadness that eats away at our courage. The Creator has given us these pleasures only to rest and recreate us, to bring our thoughts back to Him, and rejuvenate our energy to work in His service for our salvation.

> ***Tip for Sanguines:***
> *Use the innocent pleasures that you desire to rejuvenate and rest so that you can go back to work for the Lord.*

If these innocent pleasures are not sought with God as their center and giver, we are not using them as God intended. If we use them to raise our thoughts to Him, then we sanctify the secular and take a further step toward true happiness.

Pleasure, compared to happiness, is like the free taste of ice cream they give you at your favorite creamery, in comparison with a lifetime supply of ice cream. And, of course, eternal happiness is like—well, there really is nothing that we can compare it to here on earth. True happiness in this life comes from the peace of resting in His will, doing all we can to help ourselves and others to get to Heaven, and knowing, with the supernatural virtue of hope, that He will fulfill His promises.

"A certain participation of happiness can be had in this life," wrote St. Thomas Aquinas,[92] "but perfect and true hap-

---

[92] Saint Thomas Aquinas (1225–1274).

piness cannot be had in this life . . . For since happiness is a perfect and sufficient good, it excludes every evil, and fulfills every desire. But in this life every evil cannot be excluded."[93]

And that brings us to a discussion of the Melancholics of this world, who know, and often dwell upon, how perfect happiness cannot be had on earth.

---

[93] *ST* I–II. Q. 5. Art. 3.

5

The Sensitivity of St. Thérèse and the Playfulness of St. Philomena

Melancholic and Sanguine

Saint Thérèse of Lisieux—the "Little Flower"—was born the youngest of nine children, on January 2, 1873. She could easily have become spoiled and entitled, being the youngest in a wealthy family with four older sisters to dote on her, but her saintly parents, Louis and Zélie Martin, taught her a great love for Jesus. Their four youngest children all died in early childhood.

If you visit Lisieux, you can see a priest's chasuble that Thérèse embroidered, using a gown of her mother's. She created two white roses to represent her parents, five lilies for the surviving daughters, and four white lily buds for the siblings she never knew. We can see her sensitivity, subtlety, and creativity in this masterpiece. Melancholics are often delicately perceptive and deeply creative.

Little Thérèse dressed in elegant dresses and curls. She was deeply attached to her mother, who had a lovely lace-making business. When baby Thérèse was only four, her mother died of breast cancer. It broke her affectionate heart. She attached herself to her second oldest sister, Pauline, and when that one entered the cloistered Carmelite convent, Thérèse's health collapsed.

"I became so ill that, humanly speaking, there was no hope of recovery," she wrote in her autobiography. "I said things which I did not think, and I did things as though I were forced to do them in spite of myself. Most of the time I appeared delirious, and yet I am quite certain I was never for one moment deprived of my reason. Sometimes for hours together I remained in a strange kind of swoon, unable to make the slightest movement, and yet hearing everything that was said around me, even when spoken in a whisper."[94] She was miraculously cured by a family statue of Our Lady which smiled upon her. The image is now known as "Our Lady of the Smile."

After many years of wishing to be a Carmelite, she was finally allowed to enter the strict cloistered Carmel of Lisieux at the age of fifteen. Her sisters Marie, Pauline, and Celine were all Carmelites with her, while their remaining sister, Leonie, joined a different order.

St. Thérèse is best known for her "Little Way" to Heaven and her autobiography which is still in print—*The Story of a Soul.* She became the Mistress of Novices in her convent and taught the new Sisters how to make little sacrifices, prayers, and acts of love to climb the ladder to Heaven. She died of tuberculosis at the age of twenty-four, on September 30, 1897. She promised those around her that she would spend her Heaven doing good on earth.

[94] *Little White Flower*, 53–54.

In contrast to St. Thérèse's Melancholic nature, let's take a look at St. Philomena.

A Brief Biography of St. Philomena

Saint Philomena was a Christian martyr in the early 4th century. Her bones were not discovered until May 25, 1802. She could have been known and honored over the centuries like St. Agnes or St. Cecilia, but it seems that God wanted to save St. Philomena for a later time. Since the finding of her relics, she has inspired many saints and popes over the past 200 years.

The stone tablets sealing her grave were marked with arrows, an anchor, a spear, a palm, and a lily. The lily denoted virginity, and the palm martyrdom. The others were presumed to be representative of the methods used during attempts to kill her.

Some years later, St. Philomena appeared to three different people who did not know each other and revealed the facts of her life to each. She was a Greek princess, whose parents had prayed in vain for a child. A Catholic priest told them that if they would be baptized and pray to the one true God, their prayers would be answered. They did so and were blessed by the birth of Philomena (from the Latin: *Filia lumena*—Daughter of Light).

Her parents' city-state was in danger of invasion by the Roman Emperor Diocletian, and so the three traveled to Rome to beseech the emperor to leave them in peace. Unfortunately, Diocletian offered them a terrible choice—peace for their country in exchange for the hand in marriage of thirteen-year-old Princess Philomena.

Even if she had wanted to marry an older pagan man who already had wives, Philomena could not because she had promised her virginity to Jesus. Diocletian, enraged by her rejection, threw her into prison. Despite being scourged, shot with arrows, and even thrown into the Tiber River with an anchor about her neck, her faith and courage remained unshaken. As the story is told, each of Diocletian's attempts to kill Philomena failed because of miraculous intervention. That is, until she was beheaded and dispatched to glory on August 10, 302.

Let us examine these two saintly young women and what we can learn from their stories.

Saint Thérèse of Lisieux, the dear Little Flower who lived such a beautiful life, and who has brought so much inspiration to the Church since her death, was a textbook Melancholic. Her sensitivity to all the little pinpricks of life and interactions with human beings became the foundation of her Little Way to Heaven. For example, she turned her fear of spiders, and her disinclination to be splashed by dirty water while doing laundry into precious gifts she could offer the Savior whom she loved so dearly.

At the age of fourteen, her greatest wish was to become a Carmelite like her namesake St. Teresa of Ávila. She gently and tactfully broke the news to her dear widowed "Papa" and begged for his approval. With her temperament, she would never risk breaking Papa's heart by running away like her namesake did at age eighteen, 300 years earlier. This is not to say that St. Teresa of Ávila was wrong for doing what she did. God knew Teresa and Thérèse had different temperaments; He made them that way and led them by different paths to sanctity.

We are the same in Heaven as we were on earth. We are the same people but glorified. As Fr. Collin's explains:

> In the resurrection to eternal life each one's personal identity will be preserved, We have two lives; one in time, the other in eternity: but they are not disconnected. The latter life is dependent on the former, and is a sort of continuation of it, in a freer, more exalted condition. One of the things our Blessed Lord insisted on when He rose again was His personal identity; that He was the same Jesus His disciples had known so well. 'See,' He said, 'that it is I Myself.' For this too He reminded them of things He had said in His mortal life and showed Himself in familiar characteristic ways.[95]

Saints Teresa of Ávila, Thérèse of Lisieux, and Philomena all retain their personalities in Heaven, just as Christ did after His death and resurrection. The saints even answer our requests for their prayers now in the spirit of their own personalities. So, when we ask them to intercede for us before the Eternal Throne of God, sometimes the answers that come are filtered through the way they were in life. For example, some say that Saint Joseph answers prayers slowly, but very thoroughly. This may be a clue to his temperament during life.

We only know the bare bones of the biography of Saint Philomena, but through her miracles and her answers to

---

[95] Collins, *Heaven Opened*, 270.

prayers, she shows herself playful. She may have been a Sanguine—fun-loving, laughing, and answering prayers with twinkling eyes and a merry grin.

After Philomena's body was discovered and identified as the body of a girl about thirteen years old, it was reverently transferred to a church. Father Francesco di Lucia, parish priest of a little town near Naples, called Mugnano del Cardinale, traveled to Rome in 1805 with his bishop. He felt inspired to ask for the body of St. Philomena to be brought to his parish as an inspiration to his struggling congregation. His prayers were answered.

The Bishop of Potenza and Father Di Lucia rode toward Mugnano del Cardinale with her reliquary packed under the carriage seat, but Saint Philomena did not like that. Sanguines like to be in the middle of things, not shoved out of the way. No doubt the servants who packed the carriage did not realize the importance of that particular box. Even though the bishop meant her no disrespect and merely wanted the case containing her bones to be secure, she showed her displeasure by rapping him smartly on the back of the legs.

After it happened repeatedly and quite painfully, he realized that her reliquary was not being properly honored and remembered that he had even promised her that she would be given a place of honor on the trip. He and Father Francesco di Lucia moved the relics to the seat opposite them in the carriage and spent the rest of the journey praying to the little princess saint, who had bravely stood up to the mighty emperor Diocletian—the most powerful man in the world in her day.

Philomena's miracles and ways of answering prayers show us that she was probably Sanguine. She is playful and charming, and sometimes even feisty.

When St. Philomena wants it to be known that she is answering a prayer, particularly a novena, she sometimes knocks three times. This has been heard by many people, including Pope Pius IX.

"When [Pope Pius IX was] Archbishop of Spoleto he was already her devout client and earnestly spread her devotion," wrote Father Paul O'Sullivan, OP in his book, *Saint Philomena the Wonder-Worker.* "Later on, when Archbishop of Imola, he fell dangerously ill, and the greatest fears were entertained for his life. Near his bedside stood a beautiful image of his dear Saint, who was heard to rap distinctly, as she sometimes does when about to perform a great miracle. Immediately, favorable symptoms were noticed in the patient, and these speedily developed into rapid convalescence."[96] Years later, he was elected pope, and is known for his infallible declaration of the doctrine of the Immaculate Conception.

Father di Lucia, as pastor of Philomena's shrine in Mugnano del Cardinale, wrote a book of her life and miracles. When he had some two hundred or so copies left, he set one-hundred-eighty aside, and then kept one pile of about forty to give away, not wanting to run out altogether. He kept giving from that pile (of forty) for many months, not thinking of the fact that they were being miraculously multiplied, because he never ran out.

---

[96] O'Sullivan, *Saint Philomena the Wonder-Worker*, 66.

But here is where we see Philomena's playfulness. Father di Lucia had not noticed the miraculous multiplication of the books. One day, he came back to his locked room to find the books strewn all over the floor. It seems that she wanted his attention! He discovered that the ones he had set aside were still there, in exactly the number he had left them—one hundred eighty in four piles of forty-five each. In the pile that he distributed from, there were nineteen left. All well and good, except that he found seventy-two more copies strewn around the floor, and upon examining his records, he discovered that he had given away over five hundred more copies from the little pile of forty. How endearing it is to see that Philomena did not just perform the miracle to help spread the good priest's book about her; when he did not notice and thank her, she threw them all over the floor to force him to pay attention.

Cecily Hallack, in her delightful little book about Saint Philomena, writes about how the image of Saint Philomena that contains her relics in Mugnano del Cardinale has been known to open and close its eyes. "Marianna Masucci refused to believe that anyone had seen such a thing," she writes. "'How is it possible that the Saint can open her eyes when she has none beneath those closed eyelids? How could such a thing happen to a face made of paper? If she shows this wonder to others, why not to me?' To this challenge, Philomena opened her eyes, looked severely at Marianna, and shut her eyes again!"[97] Another time, a woman was praying a novena to Saint Philomena which included the plea that a certain Catholic friend would return to the Sacraments and the

---

[97] Hallack, *Wonder Worker: Saint Philomena*, 39.

fervent practice of her Faith. Saint Philomena knocked at a time when the fallen-away Catholic would hear it too. The devotee of Saint Philomena asked the friend if she had heard the knocking from the other side of the wall, and she replied, "Yes, I thought it was you. It sounded like you were knocking in irritation." Saint Philomena was the one knocking in irritation—get yourself back to Mass and the Sacraments! The friend made her Confession and received Holy Communion shortly thereafter. She has a great devotion to Saint Philomena to this day.

Tip for All Temperaments: *Find a saint whose personality resonates with your own, and ask them to intercede for you before the Throne of God.*

Let us return to Thérèse the Melancholic. On her deathbed, she said she wished to spend her Heaven doing good on earth. "After all, the angels are continually occupied with us, while yet they never cease to see the Face of God and are rapt forever in the shoreless ocean of love," she said. "Why should not Jesus permit me to do as they do?"[98]

Thérèse promised to let fall a shower of roses on those who asked her intercession with the Most High. Thousands of her devotees tell stories of her sending them actual, physical roses in answer to their prayers.

Once, a woman named Rachel made a nine-day novena to Saint Thérèse asking her intercession with God for a baby. Her friend Rose, not knowing about the novena, had a dream one night that Rachel was expecting. She called and said, "I know this is crazy, but are you expecting another baby? I had this dream."

---

[98] Morton, *St. Therese of Lisieux*, 86.

Rachel took a pregnancy test and found out that it was true. She called Rose back and said, "I asked Saint Thérèse to send me a rose. I guess *you* were the Rose!"

Another time, a young lady who had a troubled family life and had left school was calling on St. Thérèse for her intercession. She asked for a white rose as a sign of St. Thérèse's assistance. A priest arranged for an out-of-town family to let her board with them so she could return to school and get her diploma. She said, "St. Thérèse sure answered my prayers, but I never got my rose!" Then she learned that the mother she would be staying with was a Caucasian named *Rose*.

Another time, a woman was silently (and secretly) weeping in a Catholic church in a strange town where she knew no one. A stranger tapped her on the shoulder and handed her a holy card of St. Thérèse. Without a word, the stranger left. Little Thérèse had gently touched the heart of the weeping woman with her sympathy and love.

If you are a Melancholic, you have a wonderful friend in St. Thérèse. She "gets" you. She understands when your sensitive feelings are hurt, or when you are discouraged or depressed.

> ***Tip for Melancholics:*** *Know that you might have a tendency to excessive guilt and scrupulosity. Make a good Confession, and place your trust in God.*

Melancholics often struggle with guilt and scrupulosity—the tendency to see sin where there is none. The modern world tells us that the Catholic Church gives her members guilt. As usual, the secular world reverses the truth—the Church does not put guilt on us, she helps to remove it from us! Our hearts break for those who do not have the gift of confession in the Sacrament of Penance, with the assurance of God Himself through His priest, that they are forgiven. So many people drag themselves through life, burdened with the guilt of their sins, whether it is committing the sin of abortion, their cruelty to someone else, their failure as a parent, their drug abuse, or other sins. What a gift to the Melancholic, and to all of us, is the Sacrament of Penance!

After Thérèse lost her dear Mama at only four years of age, she threw herself into the arms of her big sister Pauline, and when that sister left, Thérèse almost died. Her heavenly Mother cured her, because God had great plans for the poor little rich girl from Lisieux: she had a mission to teach us all her "Little Way."

Her autobiography shows her deep sensitivity and suffering because of her Melancholic nature. As a little child, she asked her big sister every night, "Have I been good today? Is God pleased with me? Will the Angels watch over me?" She writes, "'Yes,' was the unfailing reply—were it not, I should have spent the night in tears."[99]

Maybe one would think from this, "Wow, she was such a good little girl," but it's not just that. This delicacy of thought and spirit was part of her nature. It was part of her temperament. Of course, it is a credit to her parents and her older sisters that they helped her to direct that sensitivity toward pleasing God and not just toward pleasing herself.

When she had trouble with mean classmates in school, she tells us, "Naturally timid and sensitive, I was unable to defend myself, and took refuge in tears. Neither my little Mother [her sister Pauline] nor Celine [the sister closest to

---

[99] *Little White Flower*, 36.

her in age] knew of these troubles, and as I was not advanced enough in virtue to rise above them, I suffered a great deal."[100]

She also had an amazing memory for the different hurts that she suffered. A Melancholic often remembers everything people have done to him, for years afterward. The admirable thing to do is to imitate Thérèse: forgive, even though she was unable to forget, and look at her sufferings the way God would look at them. He gives us these trials and tribulations with a loving and understanding Heart, to strengthen us, to detach us from worldly things, and to purify us for Heaven. She often wrote about how, looking back at the age of twenty-two (when she wrote the first part of her memoir), she could see God's beautiful plan through her trials and sorrows.

> ***Tip for Melancholics:*** *You will probably remember every hurt and insult, but you can imitate Thérèse by forgiving and trying to see the offenses as God does.*

Thérèse was nine when she was devastated by Pauline's departure for Carmel. Thirteen years later, she wrote: "How can I describe the anguish my heart endured! At that time the joy of sacrifice was still unknown to me. I was so weak, that I look back on it as an immense grace not to have died under a trial which to all appearances was far in excess of my strength."[101]

Her internal suffering was so great, that it dragged her body down with it. Now, someone of another temperament, particularly a Choleric, might think, "Well, for goodness' sake, child, buck up! Stop being a spoiled brat, and go enjoy your wealth and status, and the constant love and attention

[100] *Little White Flower*, 43.
[101] *Little White Flower*, 47–48.

of your father, remaining sisters, and cousins!" But it's not as easy as that for a Melancholic. She suffered greatly until she, like she says, discovered the joy of sacrifice, and Our Lord led her to her "Little Way." When she offered little splinters from the Cross to Him, they cost her a great deal. Someone who was not Melancholic may not have suffered so much from the little things that Thérèse found excruciating, but they might struggle with something else.

Thérèse was terrified by the spiders that lurked in a dusty dark corner that she was told to dust in the convent. One of the other nuns, who washed her laundry beside Thérèse in a large basin, repeatedly splashed dirty water on the fastidious Thérèse. Another nun continually fidgeted and jiggled her rosary beads during meditation, as Thérèse knelt beside her. These things upset and irritated the saint, but she found a way to offer them as little acts of love to Jesus.

> ***Tip for Melancholics:*** *When people or things irritate you, offer them as little acts of love to Jesus.*

She considered her "Little Way" an elevator to help us get to Heaven. "What she wanted was to reach out into the wide world and to tell you and me that if we really wish to please God, there is a way of doing it without undergoing special training, without asceticism, but by regarding the thousand incidents of everyday life as a thousand opportunities for trying to humble ourselves," wrote J.B. Morton.[102]

For someone who is solely Choleric, maybe a splash of dirty water or a spider in a cupboard would not be something that made him or her suffer. But there are other things that irritate a Choleric—like incompetency, for example. It

[102] Morton, *St. Therese of Lisieux*, 95.

takes great strength of will to overcome the desire to snap at someone and exercise patience instead. J.B. Morton writes, "When the will has grown rusty from disuse, the initial effort to get it working seems too great."[103]

Another time, Thérèse really wanted to be asked to do a particular task. When the Sister Portress came and invited Thérèse to help, she purposely moved very slowly. When another Sister jumped up and got to perform the choice assignment, the Portress teased Thérèse for her slowness, but Thérèse was doing another sacrifice for Jesus.

Tip for all Temperaments: *Start small. St. Thérèse said we can even pick up a pin from the ground with great love.*

She also learned from this occasion that it is easy to misjudge someone. In that moment, Thérèse was judged to be slothful and slow, but really it was an act of virtue. Let us always give others the benefit of the doubt, whenever we possibly can.

Saint Thérèse must have had a strong streak of Choleric in her temperament too, because of the iron will she exercised in the convent as this "Little Flower" grew into a spiritual giant. When she desperately wanted the consolation of a conversation with her own sisters, she would purposely approach a difficult or cranky nun and keep her company instead as an act of charity. With each little sacrifice offered to God, her will strengthened even more.

J.B. Morton tells us, "Early in infancy her capacity for warm and demonstrative affection was accompanied by incessant demands for an equally demonstrative affection in return. She was self-willed, precociously intelligent, and

[103] Morton, 97.

unreasonably sensitive. Her attractive gaiety might at any moment end in tears."[104]

But as she practiced self-control and self-sacrifice moment by moment, she became stronger and stronger in the practice of virtue. She progressed from being a pretty, petulant child to a young woman of poise, grace, and virtue.

Another proof of her Choleric strength of will can be seen through the pursuit of her vocation. Although her father gave his permission, the vicar-general, the bishop, and even the pope encouraged her to wait. This fourteen-year-old, while on a group pilgrimage to Rome, broke the rules by speaking to Pope Leo XIII when they were supposed to silently kneel at an audience. "Holy Father, if only you were to say 'yes', everyone else would be willing."

> ***Tip for All Temperaments:*** *If you strengthen your will by little acts of self-control and love for Jesus, you will have the strength to handle bigger trials.*

The pope answered, "Well, my child, you will enter if it be God's Will."[105] The young teen was pulled away by Vatican guards before she could pester the pope further. But soon after, her persistence paid off, and she was able to enter the Carmelite convent a few months after she turned fifteen.

At first, she felt that God offered her great support and consolation, but soon, He withdrew His palpable comfort so that she could prove her love. As the saying goes, "If God seems silent, remember, the teacher is always silent during the test." Thérèse experienced spiritual dryness and even doubts against the Faith in her short life, but because she

---

[104] Morton, 15.

[105] *Little White Flower*, 125.

had strengthened her will with so many little acts of love, she was able to handle the bigger tests when they came.

Saint Thérèse was an expert at taking the strengths and weaknesses of her temperament and using them for good. She remembered in her childhood that Leonie once offered Thérèse and their other sister Celine a choice from a basket of toys. Celine chose something small, but Thérèse, rather selfishly, claimed the whole basket.

Tip for all Temperaments: *Flip your faults and weaknesses upside down and use them as tools to bring you closer to Christ.*

Later in life, Thérèse likened this incident to the choice we have to make about what sacrifices to do for God. "My God, I choose all," she told Our Lord.[106] She would do all the sacrifices she possibly could, as acts of love for Him. "She took that trait in her character of which she was ashamed," writes J.B. Morton, "And made it into an instrument of sanctity. Her selfishness became self-immolation."[107]

We can all pray to St. Thérèse for help, regardless of our temperament. "Having experienced herself temptation, discouragement, unhappiness, scruples, aridity, she is compassionate with those in affliction and has words of guidance for the troubled and the doubting," writes J.B. Morton.[108]

Thérèse was assigned the position of Mistress of Novices. Although she was young herself, and some would say inexperienced, she was put in charge of the new, young nuns. Here, parents and teachers can learn from her example.

She treated each novice differently based on her temperament and the needs of her soul. She watched them, prayed for them, and taught them, as individuals.

---

[106] Morton, *St. Therese of Lisieux*, 25.

[107] Morton, 25.

[108] Morton, 107.

"One [novice] would require a certain sternness which might merely frighten or antagonize another," wrote J.B. Morton. "In one case a direct rebuke would be essential, in another, some gentler method of correction. Thérèse was an admirable judge of character and could often read thoughts."[109]

> ***Tip for Parents and Teachers of all Temperaments:*** *Every child is different. Study them and apply the appropriate help for each child.*

She learned that what worked for her, or the way she would wish to be spoken to, might not work in precisely the same way for the young women she trained. Thérèse wrote, "Our own tastes, our own ideas must be put aside, and in absolute forgetfulness of self we must guide souls, not by our way, but along that particular path which Our Lord Himself indicates."[110]

Most importantly, Thérèse always remained cheerful. The Sisters thought her life was easy and that she never suffered (and sometimes even said so). But in reality, her sweet manner came with a lot of effort, especially when people around her were irritating, tedious, or even harsh. She followed St. Francis de Sales when he said, "A sad saint would be a sorry saint."[111]

She thought of each trial or tribulation as an opportunity to show that she loved and trusted Our Lord. She trusted His will for her, and her cheerful alacrity in doing what He asked of her in that moment, proved her love and confidence in Him.

St. Thérèse also had a great devotion to Saint Mary Magdalene. Perhaps we wonder how an innocent young maiden

[109] Morton, 95.

[110] *Little White Flower*, 214.

[111] Sheed, *Saints are Not Sad*, 6.

who entered a convent at age fifteen and died at twenty-four could have anything in common with a woman who lived a scandalous life in public adultery, but Thérèse recognized a kindred spirit in the great *love* of the Magdalene. Next, we will look at the probable temperament of this passionate saint from the Gospels.

"The Magdalene, most of all, is the model I like to follow. That boldness of hers, which would be so amazing if it weren't the boldness of a lover, won the Heart of Jesus, and how it fascinates mine!"
—St. Thérèse of Lisieux[112]

---

[112] *Little White Flower*, 240.

6

St. Mary Magdalene and Her Sister St. Martha

Sanguine-Melancholic and Choleric

Saints Mary Magdalene and Martha were sisters who lived in Bethany with their brother, Lazarus, during the time of Christ. Modern-day movies portray Mary Magdalene as a prostitute, but there is no mention of that in Scripture or in ancient tradition.

The old Jewish historians say that Mary Magdalene wed a Jewish man named Pappus (or Paplius or Paphos),[113] but the marriage was unhappy. She began living an adulterous life with a pagan Roman: an unforgivable sin in the eyes of her Jewish friends and relations. As a matter of fact, in the ancient Mosaic law, she was even subject to being stoned to death. Scripture tells us that her soul became possessed by seven devils.

It is believed that she got a civil divorce from her husband (another scandal to devout Jews),[114] and went to live at her estate in Magdala, near the Lake of Tiberias. When Our

[113] Heuser, *The House of Martha at Bethany*, viii, 34.
[114] Heuser, 35.

Lord visited the home of Simon the Pharisee nearby, Mary of Magdala could not resist going to see the famous Preacher. Little did she know that the Master was calling to her heart.

Father H.D. Lacordaire, who wrote so beautifully of this saint, says that she anointed His feet with special ointment and wiped them with her hair on two different occasions. In the first incident, she made her confession of guilt and repentance, and He gave forgiveness and absolution. In the second, she was, as Our Lord explained to bystanders, anointing Him for His burial. Saint John refers to the first one in the past tense in chapter 11 of his Gospel, and then relates the second one in chapter 12.

We know from Scripture that the converted Magdalene was one of the few faithful who stood at the foot of the Cross, and she was at the Sepulcher before dawn on Easter morning. As is often said of her, she was "last at the cross, first at the tomb."

A ninth-century biographer tells us that after the first Pentecost, Mary Magdalene followed the Blessed Mother, serving her as a handmaid. Sometime later, Martha, Lazarus, and Mary Magdalene sailed to France, along with some other early Christians. After preaching the Gospel with her siblings and friends for a time, she retired to a cave called Sainte-Baume in what is now Provence. She prayed and did penance for thirty years.

Father Lacordaire writes:

> When the hour of her release drew near, tradition tells us St. Mary Magdalene was borne by angels to the spot where the Aurelian Way crosses the roads leading to

> Saint-Maximin-la-Sainte-Baume. A column, named the Saint-Pilon, reminds the traveler of this memorable event, and on its summit is a representation of the wonderful transit. A few steps farther off was the modest oratory of St. Maximin . . . On this spot the bishop awaited and welcomed the friend of his Divine Master; from his hand she received the Body and Blood of her Lord, and then fell peacefully asleep.[115]

If a Melancholic's temperament is mixed with Choleric, he or she wants everything perfect, but they want it now and in their own way. If a Melancholic's temperament is combined with Sanguine, then life at each moment is either joyful, happy, and fun, or it is deeply sorrowful and hopeless. Melancholic-Sanguines have a hard time finding the golden mean between the two extremes of joy and sadness. One can imagine what Mary Magdalene's life would have been like before she met the Master.

"We can form an idea of her ardent and impetuous nature," writes Rev. A. Galy of this saint in *The Friend of Sinners*: "Impatient before an obstacle, despising opinion and convention, ready to go to extremes, all given to passionate outbursts and painful dejection."[116] Her husband Pappus probably did not understand her temperament, which made their marriage more difficult. Without God's grace, she did not know how to control her own impulses, desires, and tantrums.

[115] Lacordaire, *St. Mary Magdalen*, 147–148.
[116] Galy, *The Friend of Sinners*, 128.

As Plato pointed out, our passions are like wild horses that will run away with our chariot if given their head. We must be strong and masterful drivers of our chariots, harnessing the mighty power of our passions to take us where we want to go: Heaven.

Trying to ascertain exactly what sins she committed before she met Our Lord only distracts us, and many novelists, from the point: she lived in mortal sin, and everyone knew it. The people in her day could be very unforgiving of those who went against the Mosaic Law. There was no turning back, no reconciliation, and no hope if you were a Jewish woman who fell from grace. We may wonder why this was not a deterrent to her. Perhaps she would echo what so many say today, "But this is how I feel!" or "It makes me feel good," or "I was following my heart."

St. Ignatius of Loyola, wise guide of the spiritual life, advises never to make big decisions in the heat of emotion—whether great joy or great sadness. If Mary Magdalene was feeling miserable in her marriage, she may have made the decision under the stress of that strong emotion, to leave her husband and move in with a Roman pagan. As we said, even if she regretted it, there was no way back to grace in the Jewish community.

Tip for Sanguines and Melancholics: *Your feelings and emotions will want to run your life. Instead, let your intellect guide your will. Seek wise advice from priests and from good Catholic mentors in your same state of life.*

On that fateful day, Mary Magdalene went to the home of Simon the Pharisee to see the renowned Preacher and Miracle-worker whom everyone was talking about. Her brother Lazarus, who had been a disciple of John the Baptist, now followed Jesus. He was probably a guest at Simon's house that day.

Saint Luke tells the story: "One of the Pharisees desired Him to eat with him. And He went into the house of the Pharisee, and sat down to meat. And behold a woman that was in the city, a sinner, when she knew that He sat at meat in the Pharisee's house, brought an alabaster box of ointment" (Luke 7:36–37).

St. Ephrem of Syria[117] hands down this tradition of Mary Magdalene's words as she purchased the ointment: "'Unfortunate woman,' I said to myself, 'How can I live any longer without obtaining my pardon and His help? But shall I dare to beseech Him from the depth of corruption which engulfs me? And yet ought I neglect to take care of my life when my physician is at hand?'"[118]

How we should echo these words when we see the priest enter the confessional and offer us the opportunity of receiving the Sacrament of Penance! How could we not want to wash our souls in His grace and redeeming Blood?

Our Lord calls us to certain places or certain people, indirectly beckoning us closer to Himself. Sometimes He calls us directly, by giving us an urge to go to daily Mass, or an invitation to go on a retreat, or to do something for someone in need for His Name's sake. Other times, it is indirect, like the desire to see a friend, pick up a certain book to read that may not be overtly a spiritual book, or go for a walk. Maybe He wants to speak to our hearts through that friend, through a line in that book, or through whom we might meet on our stroll. If we are always open to His will, and the slightest breath of the Holy Ghost, we will find our life

---

[117] Saint Ephrem of Syria (c. 306–373 AD).

[118] As quoted in Galy, *The Friend of Sinners*, 131–132.

full of little surprises, signal graces, joys, and lessons that He wants us to learn.

Tip for All Temperaments: *Be open to where God might be leading you. Ask the Holy Ghost to guide you and be docile to His inspirations.*

Patricia McGerr, in her 1960 fictional work, *Martha, Martha*, unfortunately goes into a little too much detail of Mary's life of sin, but the second half of the book, about Mary Magdalene's time with Our Lord, is beautifully and masterfully written. Writing in the voice of the saint, she says, "He looked my way, and it was as if a bright light had been thrown on my conscience and I recoiled from what I saw."[119] The Master sees us as we really are, and we should aim to do the same through the light of understanding, a Gift of the Holy Ghost.

If we are aware that we have a strong tendency to chase power and dominate others (Choleric?), or chase pleasure and be frivolous and inconsistent in virtue (Sanguine?), or be lazy and stubborn (Phlegmatic?), or be a picky perfectionist and easily discouraged (Melancholic?), then we can make a greater effort to defeat these urges. If an alcoholic does not know they have a tendency to finish the bottle once they have the first drink, they will not feel the need to fight that first sip. This knowledge and light of understanding can help us attain mastery of ourselves.

McGerr puts these words into the mouth of the Magdalene:

> It was not all as I intended. My plan was to kneel quietly behind Him, saying nothing because with Him there is no need for words, and with the spikenard anoint His Feet. He would know what was in my heart

[119] McGerr, *Martha, Martha*, 136.

> and the people would see that I had made myself His servant. But as soon as I was near Him I—It is hard to describe what I felt. It is many years since I have wept. But all at once, kneeling there, there seemed to flash before me all those whom I have hurt. Somehow—I can't explain it—They all seemed one with Him, and I had hurt Him most of all. Inside me it was as if a river had burst its banks and all my unshed tears poured forth beyond control.[120]

St. Luke continues with his account: "And standing behind at His feet, she began to wash His feet with tears and wiped them with the hairs of her head, and kissed His feet, and anointed them with the ointment" (Luke 7:38).

Father Galy beautifully records the first confession of this passionate woman with a great heart for loving as follows: "Her tears were flowing without respite, ceaselessly, a burning testimony of the stormy emotions that agitated her and which she could not keep in check. The tears arose from her heart as from a profound source where the bitter waters of a wretched past had accumulated, and where now all the joyful abundance of graces and of recent felicity had just flowed in. These tears bespoke her regret, her desolation at the wrong she had done. They were a token of affectionate, limitless thanks for the marvelous light in which her soul was now bathed."[121]

Simon the Pharisee then conceived censorious thoughts of Our Lord, wondering how He could let a public sinner

---

[120] McGerr, 137.

[121] Galy, *The Friend of Sinners*, 133.

touch His feet and defile Him. Saint Augustine[122] is known to have said that Our Lord "heard him think." What kind of arrogant, self-righteous snob would not be moved with compassion to see Mary Magdalene begging tearfully for God's forgiveness?

Father Lacordaire writes, "Few pages of the Gospel are so touching to the human heart as this one, and doubtless no other friendship ever began like this."[123] He continues, "Weeping, and neither expecting nor receiving a single word of encouragement, Mary unlooses her magnificent tresses, and making them minister to her penitence, wipes with those silky and humbled locks the Feet she has bathed with her tears. Never before had a woman's tresses been condemned, or should we say, *consecrated*, to such a ministry of tenderness and expiation."[124]

Father Lacordaire points out that St. John, the apostle of love, describes the Magdalene as, "It was that Mary who anointed the Lord with perfume, and wiped His feet with her hair."[125] In other words, this beautiful act of penitence and love was one of her greatest acts, and a defining moment in her life.

In this emotional moment, as Mary Magdalene sobs and Simon the Pharisee looks down his nose at her crouching at the Master's feet, Our Lord does not remain silent. His Heart is touched as He reads both her heart and Simon's. Mary Magdalene recognizes that He has come to bring grace

---

[122] Saint Augustine (354–430).

[123] Lacordaire, *St. Mary Magdalen*, 69.

[124] Lacordaire, 72.

[125] Lacordaire, 59.

and heal the world of sin. Simon the Pharisee mentally condemns, thinking he is superior.

The Lord speaks. "Simon, I have somewhat to say to thee." The Pharisee hypocritically says, "Master, say it" (Luke 7:40). Our Lord then told the story of one who is forgiven five hundred pence, and another who is forgiven only fifty. Simon agreed that the man who was forgiven more would love the forgiver more.

"Dost thou see this woman?" Our Lord said gently, yet His tones rang with firmness and authority. "I entered into thy house, thou gavest me no water for My feet; but she with tears hath washed My feet, and with her hairs hath wiped them. Thou gavest Me no kiss; but she, since she came in, hath not ceased to kiss My feet. My head with oil thou didst not anoint; but she with ointment hath anointed My feet. Wherefore I say to thee: Many sins are forgiven her, because she hath loved much. But to whom less is forgiven, he loveth less" (Luke 7:44–47).

The Melancholic has such a deep capacity for love. In some ways, this makes the Melancholic most like the Sacred Heart of Jesus Himself. A Melancholic does not love in a shallow, superficial way. A Melancholic is not a fair-weather friend. They feel hurts deeply, and they feel the pain of those they love.

The Master then said to Mary Magdalene, "Thy sins are forgiven thee" (Luke 7:48) and "Thy faith hath made thee safe, go in peace" (Luke 7:50).

"O my God, thou art God indeed!" exclaims Father Lacordaire in his writings of this scene. "Thy words alone have created virtues, and Thy friendship for a sinner has created saints."[126]

The self-righteous criticized her, and even censured the Master for letting her weep over His feet. He swiftly moved to her defense, telling the pompous Pharisee that she is forgiven much because she loves much. "Your sins are forgiven," the Master told her, just as He tells us in the person of His priest at the end of Confession, "Go in peace."

> ***Tip for All Temperaments:*** *Meditate on these words of Fr. Lacordaire: "O my God, thou art God indeed! Thy words alone have created virtues, and Thy friendship for a sinner has created saints."*

She hungered for forgiveness after hearing the Master speak, and as He always does, He satisfied that hunger. "Go in peace," He told her. Saint John tells us that she was freed from the power of seven devils: either literally in that she was possessed by demons, or that she was under Satan's power because she lived in mortal sin.

Many people, though of course not all, who make a general Confession experience this kind of tears. "Most sweet St. Mary Magdalene," writes E. Seton, "I place all my Confessions henceforth under thy patronage that thou mayest obtain me thine own graces of humility, perfect contrition, and burning love of my Saviour, Who receives me every time so tenderly."[127]

We can offer St. Mary Magdalene all our regular Confessions, asking her to help us to have true contrition and a firm purpose of amendment. We can also pray for her intercession for the grace of making a general Confession of our whole life.

---

[126] Lacordaire, 77–78.

[127] Seton, *Sundays in the Garden,* 43.

> ***Tip for All Temperaments:*** *Imitate Mary Magdalene's humility, contrition, and fervent love, especially when going to Confession. Ask her to help.*

A general Confession can be of two kinds: The first is a necessary one, when one who is baptized is converting from another religion, or because one has made a bad Confession (e.g., knowingly leaving out a mortal sin). The second kind is a general Confession of devotion, in which we recap all our previous Confessions to show Our Lord how really sorry we are, and to get an overview of our whole life and how we have offended the dear Master. The faithful make general Confessions during retreats, before major events in their lives such as marriage, entering the seminary, retiring from their career, and the like. The grace, contrition, and tears of repentance that wash over the soul are immeasurably beneficial on our journey to our final goal of Heaven.

Highly emotional people can surely learn control from Mary Magdalene, but a soul of any temperament can find in her story, as Seton says, humility, contrition, and fervent love. Any school-aged Catholic child can tell you what you must do to make a good Confession, including: "Be sorry for my sins; make up my mind not to sin again," but Mary Magdalene gives us a vivid, living example of this. Our Lord says that wherever this Gospel is preached, throughout the centuries and through every nation, this story will be told of her.

The narrative of her life and her fall from grace also sheds light on the age-old question, "Why would God allow this?" No doubt Mary Magdalene's family wondered how she could have strayed so far from the teachings of the Jewish religion. Perhaps they struggled with the thought of how God could have let this shame and disgrace come upon their wealthy, respectable, devout Jewish family name. Our Master knew that, far from striking her dead in her sins, allowing her time and opportunity for repentance would help her become a much greater saint than her family or sanctimonious neighbors could have believed possible. "Wheresoever this gospel shall be preached in the whole world," this story "shall be told for a memory of her" (Matt. 26:13).

Tip for All Temperaments: *Find comfort in the Sacrament of Penance. If it is a source of fear or dread for you, then ask to meet with the priest outside the confessional to discuss your concerns. This sacrament was instituted to be a solace—as it was to Mary Magdalene.*

The Master knew that the account of her sins, her expiation, and forgiveness would inspire countless souls down the centuries until the end of the world, wherever the Gospel is preached. What a way our God has of taking something bad that people do and turning it into something for their benefit!

The Sacred Heart of Jesus not only forgives our sins when we repent but takes them a step further. Father Francis P. Donnelly, SJ writes:

> [The Heart of Jesus] has not only forgiven the wrongs done to It, but by a divine refinement of mercy and charity It changed the blow that was dealt It into a benefit for the hand that dealt the blow, and conferred on Its murderers [on Calvary] the power of salvation and life everlasting in the very act in which they robbed It of life, dying for those who were killing It, saving those who were slaying It. The Blood that rushed from the Heart of Christ went speeding upon an errand of mercy, hurrying out to heal Its enemies

> and destroyers; it was warm, eternal, infinite forgiveness from the Heart.[128]

Mary Magdalene rose from her knees, from her First (and general) Confession, with a soul full of peace, joy, and gratitude. For the rest of her life, the God-Man was her sole love and all she wanted was to be near Him.

We are told in the very next chapter of the Bible that she follows Him on His preaching trips, ministering to Him. Her family's home at Bethany is the only one that we know Our Lord repeatedly visited. She can think of nothing but worshiping Him, even when her sister Martha asks her to help serve dinner (see Luke 10:38–42). She must not miss a word that falls from His sacred lips.

The beauty of Mary Magdalene's friendship and affection for the Divine Master is such that the devil cannot resist attacking it. Perhaps this is why the dragon so furiously blows his hellish breath on the precious flower of the association between the Lord and this poor sinner. If he can destroy the immaculate perfection of Our Lord's dealings with her, then he can obscure with his fiery smoke the scene of a sinner's repentance and Our Lord's generous reward. The Scripture clearly states, "Jesus loved Martha, and her sister Mary, and Lazarus" (Jn. 11:5). Yet at the same time, Our Lord does not even speak to her from the Cross as He is dying. Despite this, today's writers cast the horrible aspersion that Our Lord and Saint Mary Magdalene were *dating.* Satan just cannot ignore something so pure, so beautiful, and so comforting to poor sinners who desire forgiveness. He cannot stop it being

---

[128] Donnelly, *The Heart of the Gospel*, 141.

told everywhere that the Gospel has been preached for the past two thousand years, so he taints it with human frailty and tries to paint it as something sensual, carnal, and even scandalous. The smell of sulfur emanating from such ideas is nauseating. Our Lord and Mary Magdalene did not have a carnal relationship—she purely and chastely loved Him as her God and her Lord.

Sister Squabbles

The more we understand the temperaments of others, the more we can show helpfulness and empathy. Maybe we do not have *those* weaknesses in our temperament, but we have other shortcomings. Sisters Martha and Mary Magdalene provide an excellent example of people who, though growing up together, do not understand each other's temperaments.

> ***Tip for All Temperaments:*** *We are all created differently. The study of all four temperaments helps us to be more understanding of others.*

After cleaning up the whole house and making a fancy dinner, Saint Martha (the Choleric sister) was serving Our Lord Jesus Christ, His Mother, His Apostles, and other guests. She was frustrated and exasperated that her sister Mary was sitting at His feet the whole time, absorbing what He said. No doubt she thought, "Who does she think she is? The Queen of Sheba? She, who used to live an adulterous life with a pagan Roman, now acts like she's some sort of mystic, sitting at His feet looking at Him with soulful eyes, when she should be helping me with the dishes!"

This would be a moment that the Melancholic St. Thérèse of Lisieux would advise silence and restraining the tongue. But St. Martha, being a strong Choleric, was too outspoken for that. She spoke as calmly and respectfully as she could, but certainly with a strain in her voice.

"Lord, hast Thou no care that my sister hath left me alone to serve?" she asked. "Speak to her therefore, that she help me" (Luke 10:40).

We can see Our Dear Lord calmly and gently looking from Martha, standing with one hand on her hip and carrying a large serving plate, then to Mary, sitting on a low stool with empty hands but a full heart.

"Martha, Martha," He said gently, His repetition of her name showing His tenderness for His hostess. "Thou art careful, and art troubled about many things: But one thing is necessary. Mary hath chosen the best part, which shall not be taken away from her" (Luke 10:41–42).

Ouch! As a Choleric, she probably felt stabbed to the heart. Not only did He humiliate her and tell her that her previously sinful sister was doing better than the efficient, reputable, exemplary Martha, but He did not rebuke the Magdalene like she asked. What a huge trial for a Choleric!

Saint Martha may have wanted to thump the platter down on the table, throw up her hands and shout, with a glare at her sister, "Fine! If she's doing so great just sitting there doing nothing, then maybe I should too! Maybe the dinner will cook itself and the dishes will wash themselves! I'll choose the better part like her and do absolutely nothing too!"

Our Lord, however, was flooding her heart with grace by His very Presence in her house, as He does when He comes to us in Holy Communion. "The eyes of Jesus gazed upon her troubled countenance lovingly, while self-love and pride battled with her nobler nature," writes Katherine F. Mullany, "And grace won under the power of that sweet glance."[129]

Think of how often Our Lord turns that loving, sweet glance on us, understanding our struggles, watching us battle with what we should do and what we would really rather do, and seeing us decide between grace and pride. In the case of the dirty splashed water of St. Thérèse, she had to decide between grace and self-love. Perhaps we have to choose between grace and human respect or between grace and the bad habits entrenched in our lives from repetition.

His sweet glance is upon us, too, and His grace is sufficient for us, just as it was for St. Paul. If we turn to Him with the eyes of the spirit, we will see Him looking affectionately back at us. He watches us with the same warm, encouraging smile and loving support that a parent gives, as a child takes her first quavering steps. May we not let Him down; may grace win in our hearts as we fight these same battles against self-love and pride that the saints have been fighting for millennia!

Tip for Cholerics (and all Temperaments): *When you want to snap at someone, especially a family member, think of Our Lord's loving eyes upon you, and take a moment to calm yourself before speaking.*

Once again, we see that Our Lord defends Mary Magdalene: a former public sinner, who had scandalized her community. He defends her because of her humility and penitence. She loves and repents in silence, and never speaks up to excuse herself, because she knows she has deserved their scorn, condescension, and condemnation in the past.

[129] Mullany, *Miriam of Magdala*, 56.

On the other hand, Martha's pious diligence is not being punished by the all-wise Master. *The Life of St. Mary Magdalene and of Her Sister Saint Martha* was written in the ninth century by Rabanus Maurus. He writes of this scene: "The repetition of her name [Martha, Martha] is a sign of love. He loved both sisters with a wonderful affection—Martha, for her almsgiving and religious deeds; Mary for her unwavering contemplation."[130]

Just as Our Lord tells us in the parable of the prodigal son, He will reward, in His Infinite Justice and Mercy, both the one who repented *and* the one who never strayed but faithfully performed her duty at home.

> ***Tip for Melancholics and Cholerics:*** *Learn from the example of Martha and Mary Magdalene: Jesus is perfect action and contemplation. Neither is perfect by itself.*

"The contrast between these sister-saints," writes Father Vincent McNabb, OP in his *St. Mary Magdalen*, "has provided us almost with a literature on Mysticism. Martha seems to be the soul born with good dispositions. She trusted in her own natural powers, which in point of fact had rarely failed her. Neither St. Martha nor St. Mary Magdalene is perfect. Both are on the way. But neither has reached the end. Life is work and thought, action and contemplation. . . . Jesus is perfect action and contemplation."[131]

Cholerics like St. Martha are often right in their decisions, like Fr. McNabb says. She had good instincts. Mary Magdalene's impulses often drew her in the wrong direction in her early life, but as a Melancholic, she had the gift of sensitivity and a deep capacity for love. Our Lord

---

130 Maurus, *Life of St. Mary Magdalene*, 41.

131 McNabb, *St. Mary Magdalen*, 51.

rewards us for what we are doing right, while leading us, as a good spiritual director does, to fix the things that are not quite right.

Father McNabb continues:

> Martha is not perfection in her action; nor Mary in her contemplation Martha is largely seeking the joy of her own will. Active minds do not always ask what is needed by others but what they think is needed by others. Perfect courtesy demands that the host shall find out exactly what the guest wants and will provide it. Some hosts with hearts larger than their minds make up their mind what their guests must have and then see that they have it . . . Martha's action had too much of Martha's will and too little of the will of Jesus.[132]

A person of any temperament can fall into this trap, but Cholerics or Choleric-Melancholics have the greatest tendency in this direction.

Martha is showing a little too much of her own willfulness, pushing her own spirituality on her sister. Our Lord gently chides Martha. A modern-day example would be a busybody who tells someone who is silently praying, "It's better to get up and serve Him than to sit there in church doing nothing." Someone who belongs to every church committee and runs every church fundraiser (a Martha) might rebuke someone who goes on a retreat instead (a Mary Magdalene).

"Our Blessed Lord did not condemn Martha's *work,* but Martha's *worry,*" writes Father McNabb. "Besides her great concern was that her sister should help, not Jesus, but herself,

---

[132] McNabb, 51–52.

'That she help me.' . . . Martha is so careful for what Jesus needs that she forgets who Jesus is."[133]

Many Cholerics focus so much on what they are doing, and what they think everyone else should be doing, that they forget why they are doing it. Martha lost sight of loving Our Lord in her service to Him, she was focused on creating the perfect meal and clean house instead.

"Martha served, Mary listened and meditated," wrote Fr. Lacordaire. "Martha stood, Mary sat at the Feet of the Savior. Martha complained, Mary was silent. Between these two affections, so differently expressed, hesitation is not possible; and in declaring that of Mary preferable, Jesus gave it the preference, and promised to it the better part that should never be taken away."[134]

> ***Tip for All Temperaments:*** *Take time to meditate on the life of Jesus. Pick a thought you can come back to during the day.*

This of course, is not to say that a dad working three jobs to support the family, or a mother homeschooling eight children has the "worse part" because he or she cannot spend hours a day before the Blessed Sacrament. The Divine Master gives us different missions in life. We can always keep the contemplative state in our hearts—preparing a little place for Our Lord in our daily meditation, like Saint Francis de Sales suggested, that we can return to during the day. If we spent our twenty minutes of meditation this morning on the home at Bethany, for example, then throughout the day, we could return there mentally in just a few seconds, to once again consecrate our daily duty to the Divine Master. He sees; He smiles; He rewards us.

---

133 McNabb, 49, 50.

134 Lacordaire, *St. Mary Magdalen*, 58.

A Possible Meditation

Think of the Magdalene sitting at the Master's feet in the house of Bethany, her traditional Jewish home with her sister Martha and brother Lazarus. She gazes up at His face, soaking up His every expression and meaningful gesture, capturing every word in her heart, so that she can treasure it forever.

Think about how we listen with fervor and attention to a good priest talking about the spiritual life or giving a retreat, especially when we know the priest is going to leave us or the retreat will end. Let us make the most of these precious moments!

Let it spark your imagination, to see how intensely the Magdalene felt as she looked into the face of Jesus Christ Himself, sitting at her kitchen table in Bethany at the end of dinner. Who would have wanted to get up and help Martha with the dishes? Think of what it would have been like to hear Heaven described, in your own language, by the One who made it! Think of what it would have felt like to look into those eyes, and see those eyes look back at you—deep into your soul—filled as they were with the utmost understanding of your weaknesses, your sufferings, your sorrows, and your triumphs! To hear His voice say your name with love!

We read in Saint John's Gospel, "Now Jesus loved Martha, and her sister Mary, and Lazarus" (Jn. 11:5). They were His personal friends, in spite of Martha's Choleric-Melancholic bossiness and in spite of Mary's letting her emotions run away with her. He understood them. He never condoned or approved Mary Magdalene's immoral lifestyle, but He understood her weakness, and believed in her ability to correspond to grace, when He said, "Go in peace" (Luke 7:50).

That's the ticket—the ticket to understanding the temperaments and the ticket to Heaven. God understands our weaknesses; we should try to understand them too. We are not justifying our weaknesses, nor excusing them, but understanding them so that we may overcome them and build on our strengths.

The Master believes in us. He believed that the Sanguine, zoom-eek (always zooming forward, or screeching to a halt) Peter could be "the Rock" upon which He built His Church. "Simon, Simon, behold Satan hath desired to have you, that he may sift you as wheat: But I have prayed for thee, that thy faith fail not: and thou, being once converted, confirm thy brethren" (Luke 22:31–32). Sanguines, like Peter, who convert have a much harder time being consistent and persevering in the path of virtue than Melancholics. But Our Lord prayed for him, that his faith would not fail. And look at what Peter became, because Christ prayed for him and believed in him!

Let us also believe in those around us who are trying to do their best to become saints. Let us not be the voice of discouragement, saying, "Well, I'm sure you won't be able to keep your temper this time; you never do;" or "You probably won't be able to keep out of the bar this weekend; you get drunk every Friday night." Let us pray for our neighbors and believe in their capacity for good. Our Lord believed that the notorious public sinner Mary Magdalene could reform her life and sin no more. He gives us the warmth of His smile when we get discouraged, or the smile of those He sends to us for our consolation. He believes that we too can, through the strength of His grace, achieve great things for His glory, finish the race, and win the prize.

Think of the glow and consolation that would have come when Our Lord Jesus Christ smiled down at the weeping Magdalene at His feet as she mourned, "How could I have done these things? I'm no good! What if I fall into these sins again? I can't trust myself!"

> ***Tip for Melancholics:*** *Criticism and negative remarks will come easily to you—try to change your thoughts and words to encourage and uplift others.*

He looked deep into her eyes, and said, "Mary, come to Me with your burdens, and I will refresh you. For My yoke is easy, and My burden light. He that believeth in Me shall have life everlasting" (see Matt. 11:30 and Jn. 6:47).

Her temperament needed an intense personal love for Jesus to put her on the road to Heaven. The temperament of someone like Thomas Aquinas—many believe him to have been Phlegmatic—needed to fall in love with God through his intellect. Mary Magdalene needed a friend, a confidant, a loving Master (whom she called, *Rabboni* or "dearest Master"), to unite her heart, intellect, and will to the Almighty Trinity.

What do you need to focus on, to unite yourself to Him? Think on that, and then choose a thought to treasure throughout the day.

Mary Magdalene's Progress

When a Melancholic is moved to repent and make changes in his or her life, the immediate challenge is to follow through and show firm purpose of amendment. Not only does Mary

Magdalene show us how to repent and make a good Confession, but she also shows exceptional follow-through and perseverance—thereby becoming one of the greatest saints in the Heavenly Kingdom.

Saint John, the Apostle of Love and the Sacred Heart, relates to us the second anointing that Mary Magdalene performed for her Savior, in the twelfth chapter of his Gospel, "Jesus therefore, six days before the pasch, came to Bethania, where Lazarus had been dead, whom Jesus raised to life. And they made Him a supper there: and Martha served: but Lazarus was one of them that were at table with Him." Notice that Martha has advanced in the spiritual life too, and she does not complain this time that Mary is not helping with the dishes. The Gospel continues, "Mary therefore took a pound of ointment of right spikenard, of great price, and anointed the feet of Jesus, and wiped His feet with her hair; and the house was filled with the odor of the ointment" (Jn. 12:1–3).

When Judas complained—because he wanted the price of the expensive lotion in the communal purse so he could "borrow" from it—Our Lord defended her again. "Let her alone, that she may keep it against the day of My burial" (Jn. 12:7). Little do the others know that Our Lord will be giving His life for all mankind in the next week. He was in the prime of His life, a strong, handsome Man of thirty-three, and it was the day before the triumph of Palm Sunday. None of His followers expected Him to die the next week, as St. Alphonsus de Ligouri says in his *The Way of the Cross*, the "ignominious death of the Cross."

"Christ had but six more days of mortal life," writes Father Lacordaire. "And in a few hours He must enter as king into that city where He would shortly expire as its God. Saint John has, in a special manner, noticed this moment's rest in Bethany, ere the Son of Man began to tread the way to Calvary."[135]

Mary Magdalene, however, had a premonition that He would not be with them much longer. She did not fully understand His divine mission yet, but as a Melancholic, she was sensitive and perceptive.

"Her tenderness, suffused with new light," says Father Lacordaire, "reveals to her that this repast has about it the nature of a farewell, and the end is near."[136] We would say she "felt it in her bones" that she was not going to have the consolation of His Divine Presence much longer. When we love someone with every fiber of our being, we sometimes feel when that person is in danger. She did not understand why: she did not yet know that His purpose in taking a human nature was to lay down His life for His friends.

Father Lacordaire beautifully describes her as she comes into the dining room with her alabaster jug of perfume.

> Three years of grace had passed over her brow, and sanctity had enveloped her with a divine halo. She enters, breaks the alabaster, and pours its perfume on her Savior's Head. She breaks the alabaster because she knows that all is consummated, and that never more shall the Savior receive from human hands a similar homage. This act of despair and prophetic love accomplished,

[135] Lacordaire, 88–89.
[136] Lacordaire, 90.

> Mary remembers her former baseness, and, running to the feet of Jesus, pours on them the remnant of the perfume, and wipes them with her tresses. But the Gospel names no tears. Once more shall she shed them, but at another time and another place. Now strength and composure are needed; it is no longer the hour of pardon, nor yet the hour of the tomb.[137]

See how grace, and following Our Lord, have transformed her! She has gained some control of her emotions. She still does something poetic and beautiful and prophetic: something that appeals to the soul of every Melancholic. But she is no longer sobbing emotionally over His feet. She is calm, composed, filled with grace. She has spent time with Our Lord and His grace-filled Mother, and it shows.

Naturally, when her brother Lazarus became ill, she thought of the Master immediately. For whatever reason, she was not with Jesus at this time. Maybe she was nursing her sick brother. In *Martha, Martha*, McGerr paints Lazarus as a sickly child, who was diligently cared for by his two sisters. Since the Scriptures do not record the nature of his illness, we are left to speculate. When it became severe, Martha and Mary Magdalene sent a message to Our Lord. "His sisters therefore sent to him, saying: Lord, behold, he whom thou lovest is sick" (Jn. 11:3).

What a beautiful, confident prayer! They speak with the comfort and ease of friends, yet respectful, loving friends. They know He can fix the problem; they know He will want to fix the problem; and they remind Him of His love for this person.

---

[137] Lacordaire, 90–92.

Since Martha was probably a combination of Melancholic and Choleric, and her sister Mary was Sanguine-Melancholic, it's possible that either or both of their parents (or grandparents) were Melancholic, as temperaments are most often genetic.

They knew in their hearts where to go for help, and they trusted in His love and His friendship for their family. When we consecrate our families to the Sacred Heart of Jesus, we can trust in His love and friendship for *our* families.

Our Lord said that Lazarus's sickness was "not unto death" (Jn. 11:4) which made them think that Lazarus would not die. Just because God knows what is best for us, and comforts us that everything will be all right, does not mean that the thing we fear the most will not happen. Rather, it means that God will make all things work for good (see Rom. 8:28). Think of the comfort and consolation that Christians down through the centuries have received from the account of the raising of Lazarus! Many converts were also made at the time from this miracle.

Our Lord purposely waited a couple more days to answer their prayers. "And I am glad, for your sakes," He told the Apostles, "That I was not there, that you may believe: but let us go to him" (Jn. 11:15). His followers warned Him that the Jews there wanted to stone Him to death, but Our Lord exemplified going forward to do our duty in spite of everything. He showed us an example of fulfilling the duty of charity toward our neighbor.

Saint Thomas the Apostle, who has the sorry reputation of being "doubting Thomas," here showed one of his strengths. He exclaimed to the others, "Let us also go, that we may die with him!" (Jn. 11:16). Thomas may have been cautious and doubting when he was disillusioned by Our Lord's crucifixion and death, but he was not lacking in courage or decisiveness. When Our Lord showed His wounds to Thomas in the Upper Room, Thomas once again showed his conviction and earnest resolution.

Saint John gave us a brushstroke of the scene that Our Lord found when He arrived in Bethany. The neighbors had all come in to offer their condolences and mourn with Martha and Mary. As soon as He was seen on the road outside the town, Martha ran to meet Him, but Mary sat at home.

McGerr offers the explanation that Martha happened to be on the roof of their flat Palestinian home then and caught a glimpse of Him. McGerr suggests that Mary just did not know that He was coming. This, of course, is very possible, because Scripture merely says, "Martha therefore, as soon as she heard that Jesus had come, went to meet Him: but Mary sat at home" (Jn. 11:20). It is not stated whether Mary knew He was there or not.

> ***Tip for All Temperaments:*** *When we pray, Our Lord gives us one of three answers:*
> *1. Yes,*
> *2. Not right now,*
> *or*
> *3. I have something better in mind.*

Mary Magdalene also may have been overcome by her own grief. She may have been prostrated in tears and sobs over the loss of her brother, and she may have felt hurt that Our Lord had not saved Him. She had not completely lost her trust in Him, but she may have been overwhelmed by her emotions and hurt feelings. Sometimes we are swamped by sad feelings that Our Lord does not seem to be listening to our prayers, but Our Lord's plan is always better than ours! If they had only known that

Our Lord was going to perform this magnificent miracle that would be retold down through the ages, they would have cheerfully agreed to His plan. If He had said to them clearly, "I need to let your brother die and be put in the grave for a few days, so that I can prove my Divinity and restore him to you, more healthy than ever," they would have agreed with alacrity. But Our Lord did not do that. He wants us to trust Him and to have faith that His plan is always something better than we could have imagined.

When we pray for something, Our Lord gives us one of three answers: the first is, "Yes;" the second, "Not yet;" or the third, "I have something better in mind." In this case, Martha and Mary received the third answer to their prayer.

Mary probably was so absorbed in her own sorrow, that she did not hear that Our Lord had been seen in the distance. But Martha, the Choleric-Melancholic leader-type, ran out of town to greet Our Lord on the road and respectfully rebuke Him. "Lord, if Thou hadst been here, my brother had not died" (Jn. 11:21). So often we think that if we are having a trial or tribulation, that God has abandoned us, that He is not here with us. "But," she continued with inspired persistence, "Now I also know that whatsoever thou wilt ask of God, God will give it Thee" (Jn. 11:22). There follows a beautiful exchange between the Master and Martha.

"Thy brother shall rise again," He said, to test her (Jn. 11:23).

"I know that he shall rise again, in the resurrection at the last day" (Jn. 11:24). Perhaps she felt a movement of impatience here, thinking, "I *know* he will rise again, thousands of years from now, when we all will. But You could have saved him *now*!" Remember, Choleric-Melancholics want it done their way now, and they want it done perfectly.

"I *am* the Resurrection and the life: he that believeth in me, although he be dead, shall live: And every one that liveth, and believeth in Me, shall not die for ever. Believest thou this?" (Jn. 11:25–26, emphasis added). Ah, some of the most beautiful words ever recorded in Scripture!

"Yea, Lord, I have believed that thou art Christ the Son of the living God, who art come into this world" (Jn. 11:27). She believed it, she expressed it beautifully, yet Saint Martha still had to work on taking her faith to the next step. Remembering when Martha reproves Our Lord, "Hast Thou no care that my sister hath left me alone to serve?" (Luke 10:40), Father McNabb wrote, "She has not yet broken out of the sphere of human motives into that of divine faith. She is on the road towards true faith but has not attained it. She is with the beginners who think that they give to God, rather than receive."[138] And when Our Lord commanded that the stone be drawn back from the tomb, she was still eminently practical and felt the need to remark that it has been four days and therefore her brother "stinketh" (Jn.11:39).

Martha went back to find Mary, and told her quietly, "The Master is come, and calleth for thee" (Jn. 11:28). In Ireland, there is an Adoration chapel, with a beautiful wall outside it. The stonework contains tablets that record these words, in many different languages: "The Master is here and is calling for you." Melancholics probably find it the easiest of all to go visit Our Lord in the Blessed Sacraments to keep the Master company and find strength in carrying their own crosses. But

---

[138] McNabb, *St. Mary Magdalen*, 50.

all of us must find time to do it—the busy Choleric, the distracted Sanguine, and the unmotivated Phlegmatic too.

We have already said that Mary Magdalene was happiest and most comforted in His presence, so it is no surprise that as soon as she knew He was there and wanted her to come, she hurried to Him and cast herself humbly in the dirt at His feet.

> ***Tip for All Temperaments:*** *When in sorrow, flee to His presence.*

Father Lacordaire writes:

> It is Jesus Who calls for Mary and desires that she shall witness what He is about to do. And Mary, so soon as she hears of the Master's coming, runs and falls at His Feet. Martha stood, but Mary throws herself at the Feet of Him whom she loves. Her words are [the same as] those of her sister, "Lord, if Thou hadst been here, my brother had not died." But Jesus makes no reply and demands from her no act of faith. He knows that she believes; the sight of her tears overcomes Him, and He weeps.[139]

Fr. Lacordaire gives us the lesson here: "We see that Mary possessed a deeper humility, a livelier faith, and a greater influence over the Heart of Jesus."[140]

Our Lord is all things to all temperaments. He weeps with the Melancholics, He rejoices with the Sanguines, He gets things done with the Cholerics, and He seeks peace with the Phlegmatics. He is never outdone in what is good. He is not too emotional, weeping all the time. He chose to weep seldom

[139] Lacordaire, *St. Mary Magdalen*, 55–56.

[140] Lacordaire, 56.

in the Gospel, but He did do it. He is not too bossy, running over the free will of those around Him. He sometimes spoke strongly, throwing the money-changers out of the temple or telling Peter, "Go behind me, Satan" (Matt. 16:23). He is not too frivolous, but did take the time to hold the children in His lap and embrace them. He is not too slothful, but He rested at Bethany with His friends to recreate and comfort His soul before His passion and death for mankind.

How He loves to spend time with His friends! Let us be those friends to Him now—let our homes and our hearts be another Bethany for the Divine Master to visit. Let Him know He will be loved, consoled, and eagerly welcomed in our homes and in our hearts. Like Martha hurried to fix His favorite foods, let us hurry to practice the virtues for Him. As she put flowers on the table for Him, let us put forward our sacrifices and little acts of love. As Mary sat at His feet and listened to Him, let us keep some silence in our hearts to hear His word, and sometimes spend a holy hour with Him in front of the Blessed Sacrament.

He asked Martha and Mary to show Him where they had laid His friend Lazarus. Then, just as He had raised Mary Magdalene's soul from the death of sin, He raised her brother from the death of this mortal life. "Lazarus, come forth!" (Jn. 11:43).

Our Lord's Crucifixion and Resurrection

We may well believe that before and after the Crucifixion, Mary Magdalene ministered to the Mother when she could not be with the Son, and learned feminine virtue and balance from the greatest Mary of all. What a great influence the immaculate Mother of God would have been on the tempestuous, emotional, stormily-weeping, flirtatiously laughing, Mary Magdalene! Mother Mary would have shown her how to retain her feminine dignity and loveliness, while living a life of purity and peace of heart.

"In [Our Lady's] lifetime," writes Father Gaspar Gilli, "She had already called many virgins to follow her, who became her inseparable companions; among others, St. Martha and St. Marcella. But it was also through her means that St. Mary Magdalene, who had been the scandal of Jerusalem, was enrolled after her conversion under the standard of virginal purity, and became like a brilliant crystal vase, capable of receiving and containing the most precious waters of grace."[141]

Rabanus Maurus (d. 856) wrote that, after the Descent of the Holy Ghost, "Mary Magdalene adhered with unspeakable devotion to the glorious Virgin Mary as Queen of Heaven and Mother of the Eternal King. She served as her maid with wonderful affection, giving herself over to supernal contemplation with her, and frequently sharing in the angelic visions and visitations she enjoyed."[142]

Our Lady is such a beaming example of control of her emotions. She felt everything a mother's heart can feel—joy at His birth, fear at the prophecy of Simeon, terror from losing Her Son in the temple for three days, deep grief during His passion, triumph at His resurrection. But she never

---

[141] Gilli, *The Month of Mary*, 77.

[142] Maurus, *Life of St. Mary Magdalene*, 88.

threw herself down in a wild fit of weeping, or fainted, or in any way showed uncontrollable emotion. "Now there stood by the Cross of Jesus, His Mother, and his Mother's sister, Mary of Cleophas, and Mary Magdalene," (Jn. 19:25) writes St. John, who was an eyewitness. He did not write "there swooned" or "there, lying on the ground gasping with sobs while everyone felt sorry for her." He wrote, there *stood* the Mother of Jesus, an incomparable example of how to feel, love, and mourn deeply, with dignity and control.

Our emotions and feelings can so easily rule us, especially if we are Melancholic or Sanguine. Let us learn from Our Lady's perfection, and Mary Magdalene's repentance and vast improvement in control, to master our own passions as they did.

On the other hand, if we are Choleric or Phlegmatic, we may not feel like weeping tears of remorse, love, and sorrow. Maybe we even feel disdain for those who weep. It is called the "gift of tears;" not everyone has it. The most important thing is to will our repentance, will our contrition, try to make reparation, and will our firm purpose of amendment as the Magdalene did. All her tears would have been mere emotion and pure show if she had not made a radical change of life and avoided sin and the near occasions of sin.

> ***Tip for All Temperaments:*** *When we are inclined to emotional outbursts of sorrow, anger, or any other passion, let us try to find the balance that Jesus and His Mother Mary showed. What would they do?*

At His crucifixion, Mary Magdalene showed that she had learned to combine contemplation with action. She followed Him to Calvary, stayed beside His Mother at the foot of the Cross, and then followed Him to the sepulcher.

She obeyed the Jewish law by going home for the Saturday Sabbath, probably with Our Blessed Mother to John's house, but then was the first one to hurry back to the tomb on Sunday morning.

Father Lacordaire wrote that, on Calvary, Our Lady represented all virgins, Mary of Cleophas and Salome represented Catholic wives and mothers, and Saint John represented all good Catholic men—lay or religious. The Magdalene represented the innumerable sinners whom He was washing in His Precious Blood at this moment and for all eternity, through the Holy Sacrifice of the Mass.[143]

Very early on Easter morning, Mary Magdalene (she is mentioned first in all four Gospels) made her way to the tomb with oils and spices to, for the third time, anoint her Savior. She did not go to the tomb because she knew it was the day of His resurrection, but because this was her first opportunity, due to the Mosaic Law, for her to go visit His grave and pay Him her final respects. Not only was she being active, but she was the *most* active of all because she was inspired by the true charity which He had taught her. He had infused charity into her soul during her time of contemplation at His feet.

When she arrived, she found the tomb empty, and her mind went blank. She forgot the Old Testament prophecies, she did not remember the hints He gave His followers, all she could do was burst into tears and think, "He's gone!" Sometimes our emotions obscure what we should be noticing, and sometimes Our Lord allows certain things to be hidden from our eyes. This is probably what happened when

[143] Lacordaire, *St. Mary Magdalen*, 100–101.

Our Lady "lost" Jesus for three days. Ordinarily, she would hardly have set out from the Temple in Jerusalem without being *absolutely sure* of where her Divine Son was, and with whom He was traveling. Sometimes God allows things to be hidden from our small human minds so that we do not realize something we ordinarily would have. It is, once again, part of His plan to bring about a greater good.

We read in Holy Scripture that Mary Magdalene got up in the dark to hurry back to His tomb. She arrived just as daylight was streaking the sky. In chapter 20, Saint John writes: "And on the first day of the week, Mary Magdalene cometh early, when it was yet dark, unto the sepulcher; and she saw the stone taken away from the sepulcher. She ran, therefore, and cometh to Simon Peter, and to the other disciple whom Jesus loved, and saith to them: They have taken away the Lord out of the sepulcher, and we know not where they have laid him" (Jn. 20:1–2).

Now the fact that she says "*we* know not where" confirms what the other evangelists say—that some of the other devout ladies were with her. Matthew mentions the other Mary, the mother of James; Mark mentions the two of them, plus Salome; and Luke says Joanna, the wife of Herod's steward, was also there. Mary Magdalene, who had now become more active in His service, ran to tell Peter. The other women, though, Saint Mark says, "fled from the sepulcher. For a trembling and fear had seized them: and they said nothing to any man; for they were afraid" (Mark 16:8).

Peter the Sanguine, John the Melancholic, and Mary Magdalene the Melancholic-Sanguine ran back to the tomb. They all reacted according to their temperament and character.

John was younger than Peter, so he ran faster and got there first. We know this from his own eyewitness account in John chapter 20. He tells us that he stooped down and saw the cloths lying. Although tombs were built above ground, one had to bend low to look inside. The fact that he did not enter the tomb right then indicates his nature. He either felt awe and reverence and wanted to think about what he had seen and process it (as most Melancholics would have done), or he was being *sensitive* and *respectful* of Peter's primacy and wanted to let him go first.

Peter then hurried up, panting, and being Sanguine, rushed right in to see what had happened. Then John followed him in, and seeing the shroud and other cloths, he "saw and believed" (Jn. 20:8). Peter was not as deep a thinker as John and was still confused. Saint John tells us that they both left. Then Our Lord chose to enact one of the most comforting scenes in the Holy Scripture: "But Mary stood at the sepulcher without, weeping. Now as she was weeping, she stooped down, and looked into the sepulcher, and she saw two angels in white, sitting, one at the head, and one at the feet, where the body of Jesus had been laid. They say to her: Woman, why weepest thou? She saith to them: Because they have taken away my Lord; and I know not where they have laid him" (Jn. 20:11–13).

"The Angels were there," writes E. Seton, "ready to help, as they ever are, the ardent seeker after Jesus. Lady, why weepest thou? They asked gently, wishing, no doubt, to give their Risen Lord, ready at that moment to manifest Himself, the pleasure of hearing her faithfulness proclaimed once more; asking, also, as it were, in sweet Angelic surprise that there should be tears in a lover of Christ on the morning of His Resurrection."[144]

Tip for Melancholics: It's often hard for you to "let things go"—use this to attach yourself firmly to Christ.

Instead of marveling at the fact that two mighty messengers from Heaven just appeared to her, she can only think of Our Lord and His absence. Her singleness of purpose, something that is very strong in a Melancholic's nature, is pointed in the right direction—at Jesus Himself. Like Peter, James, and John after the Transfiguration, they "lifting up their eyes saw no one but only Jesus" (Matt. 17:8). It is very hard for Melancholics to "let things go," so if they use this to attach themselves firmly to Christ, they will never leave Him by sin.

She turns away from the angels, who, Saint Matthew tells us, had countenances like lightning and raiment like snow. The Master rewards her singleness of purpose, but first He wants to hear it from her one more time—whom does she seek?

"When she had thus said, she turned herself back, and saw Jesus standing; and she knew not that it was Jesus. Jesus saith to her: Woman, why weepest thou? Whom seekest thou? She, thinking it was the gardener, saith to him: Sir, if thou hast taken him hence, tell me where thou hast laid him, and I will take him away.

"Jesus saith to her: Mary. She turning, saith to him: Rabboni (which is to say, Master)" (Jn. 20:14–16).

Imagine the wonder and joy that flooded her heart when she heard that familiar voice speaking her name in the tone she remembered so well! God said to Moses, "I know thee by

[144] Seton, *Sundays in the Garden*, 41.

name, and thou hast found favor in My sight" (Ex. 33:12). He knows each of us by name, for we are His sheep. We know His voice, and He calls us by name. In that beautiful moment of unspeakable joy, Mary Magdalene was rewarded magnificently for everything she had suffered. He recompensed her for her sorrowful searching for Him in humility and love. She thought she could render Him last services by using sweet spices on His poor, crushed, dead body, but instead, He brought her joy and resurrection.

> ***Tip for All Temperaments:*** *When Jesus floods your heart with consolation, store it away in your heart or journal it for when the going gets tough.*

He then said to her, "do not touch Me," also translated as "do not hold Me back," for He had not yet ascended to His Father in Heaven. Either way, He seemed to be telling her that instead of clutching His feet and weeping out her tears of joy, she needed to get up and do something in His service. Sometimes we feel that way at the end of Mass or a retreat. Can we just stay here and feel these consolations and happy, peaceful thoughts forever? No, we must get up off our knees and go do what He wants us to do.

"She is now risen above a servant cleansing His Feet, and has become an apostle carrying His message," writes Father McNabb.[145] The Lord gave her a beautiful message. All through His three years of preaching, He talked about "His Father," but now the disciples had become His brethren. The gates of Heaven are open once again, and God the Father is our Father too. Our Lord told her: "But go to my brethren, and say to them: I ascend to my Father and to your Father, to my God and your God. Mary Magdalene cometh, and

[145] McNabb, *St. Mary Magdalen*, 67.

telleth the disciples: I have seen the Lord, and these things he said to me" (Jn. 20:17–18).

After His Ascension

When it was time for the little band of the first Christians to go forth and teach all nations, St. Peter assigned them to Gaul, or what is now France. "The venerable hostess of the Son of God, the blessed Martha; her most reverend brother Lazarus, then Bishop of Cyprus; and her sister, following in her footsteps, together with the blessed Marcella, a woman of great devotion and faith, the handmaiden of Martha,"[146] were sent to France, according to Rabanus Maurus. Maximin, Parmenas, Trophime, and Eutropius went too, across the Mediterranean Sea to the city of Marseilles. This author says that Saint Martha's maid, St. Marcella, was the one who cried out to Our Lord, "Blessed is the womb that bore Thee, and the breasts that nourished Thee!"[147]

Some say that when the Jews began persecuting the Christians, the saints of Bethany and their friends were put in a boat without oars and exiled. Then God brought them to France to evangelize. Either way, we know they landed in what is now southern France, probably near the present town of Saintes-Maries-de-la-Mer ("the holy Marys by the Sea").

Parmenas and Martha went to Avignon. Lazarus became the bishop of Marseilles, where his relics are still revered. Mary Magdalene went with Archbishop Maximin to Aix-en-Provence. He was her spiritual director. Later, she went up

---

[146] Maurus, *Life of St. Mary Magdalene*, 92.

[147] Maurus, 92.

the mountain to an isolated cave, La-Sainte-Baume, where she is revered to this day. Tradition tells us that when she arrived there, St. Michael the Archangel appeared and drove the devil out of the cave (now that's a house blessing!). Then he used his spear to strike the rock, and a fountain of water burst forth for her use. Pilgrims climb the mountain and visit her cave in the mountainside, a breathtakingly beautiful place to be silent and pray. Truly, she is a patroness not only of penitents but of those who pray and meditate.

After thirty years of prayer and penance, she was reunited with the Savior who had so lovingly called her name in the Easter garden. She is buried at Saint-Maximin-la-Sainte-Baume, and her skull can be seen in a beautiful gold reliquary.

As Katherine F. Mullany compares the happy meeting in the Easter garden to the joyful reunion of Our Lord and Mary Magdalene at her death: "Now, she must soon part from Him, to live long years of penance far away—with only the memory of this meeting to make life bearable; but, then,—when He shall come for her—the ecstasy of her greeting shall sound through all Eternity in gladness: 'Rabboni: dearest Master!'"[148]

Meanwhile, her sister St. Martha eventually made her way to Tarascon, where she is now buried. The Latin inscription over the crypt can be translated, "Now no longer troubled."

One day, Archbishop Maximin, St. Trophime from Arles, and Bishop Eutropius all came to see Martha. She received them and served them, which was her specialty, having repeatedly received and served Our Lord Himself in the flesh at her home in Bethany. The saintly bishops dedicated

---

[148] Mullany, *Miriam of Magdala*, 100.

a church for her. After the ceremony, she served them again, and according to Rabanus Maurus, she changed water into wine after the wine ran out. Every year after her death, the bishops celebrated that day.[149]

Rabanus Maurus tells us that Saint Martha received a revelation of her own impending departure from this life. "Calling her own to her, the blessed Martha foretold to them the day of her passing in the coming year, and for the space of that entire year she lay in all her nobility on her bed of brushwood, consumed by a fever as gold is refined in the furnace."[150]

The night before St. Martha's death, her sister St. Mary Magdalene who had recently died, appeared to her and encouraged her. Then Our Lord appeared and said, "Behold, here I am, to Whom you once ministered with great devotion out of your own means; to Whom you showed a most gracious hospitality; for Whom you have done many good deeds since my Passion in the persons of my people; to Whom you once said, prostrated in reverence: 'I believe You are the Christ, the Son of the Living God, Who has come into this world.' Come, then, My hostess, come out of your exile. Come, and you shall receive your crown."[151]

Again, we see that, not only is Mary Magdalene rewarded by the Lord for her dramatic repentance, but Martha is rewarded for her faithful service. As a Choleric-Melancholic, she got things done, and she did them right. She did not need to be defended by Our Lord to her critics, for she had a spotless reputation and was highly respected.

---

[149] Maurus, *Life of St. Mary Magdalene*, 105.
[150] Maurus, 106.
[151] Maurus, 109–110.

Martha had made Bishop Fronto promise to do her requiem. When she died, Our Lord appeared to him and said, "My son, go and fulfill what you promised. Celebrate the funeral rites of My hostess Martha."[152] Then he was miraculously transported there to offer her funeral Mass!

Our Lord generously rewards the littlest things we do for Him. How much more will He reward those who dedicate their lives to His service, whether religious or lay, whether in innocence like Martha, or repentance like Mary Magdalene. This true friend of the home at Bethany "gives light to the understanding, strength to the will, unsurpassing peace to the heart, joy compatible with the greatest tribulation,"[153] writes Father Galy. "His great Heart is able to realize all dreams, to fulfill all desires. Let us attach ourselves more and more to Him, and while expecting the immense joy which will be the reward of our fidelity, let us listen to His words of truth, follow His way, live His life."[154]

---

[152] Maurus, 112.

[153] Galy, *The Friend of Sinners*, 192.

[154] Galy, 193.

7

St. Thomas Aquinas: "The Dumb Ox"?

Phlegmatic

St. Thomas Aquinas was born between 1225 and 1227, and he died in 1274. Few people in the history of the Church have influenced the written word as much as he did, in the realms of religion and philosophy. He is known as the Angelic Doctor, due to his great wisdom and unassailable purity.

His parents were Count Landulf and Countess Theodora, both of noble blood, accustomed to living in Italian medieval castles. Around the time that Thomas was born, St. Francis of Assisi died, and St. Louis IX became King of France. He had two brothers and three sisters, though all did not live to adulthood.

When Thomas was five, his parents sent him to Monte Cassino, the famous abbey of St. Benedict, to be raised and educated by the Benedictines. His parents had high hopes that their boy, with his great potential and noble blood, would become the Abbot of this great monastery with all its lands and holdings. Thomas's uncle was the Abbot when the boy arrived.

But as the years passed, great political events raged around Monte Cassino, battles (yes, even military ones) between the pope and the emperor. When Thomas was twelve, he had to go home because of a vicious attack on the Abbey. Archbishop Vaughan, in his *The Life and Labours of St. Thomas of Aquin*, tells us that while the Abbot was meeting with the Emperor in an effort to have peace, "a band of soldiers, by that same Emperor's command, forced their way into Monte Cassino, laid violent hands upon the monks, drove some of them into the mountains; and murdering the rest, in the name of their master, took possession of the Abbey."[155]

Thomas went briefly home to his family in Loreto, and then he was sent to continue his education in Naples. Here, the young Benedictine came in contact with the recently founded Dominican Order. The combination of prayer, study, and preaching appealed to the brainy young student. He joined the Dominicans.

His family, particularly his mother and two older brothers, was outraged. They chased him from Naples to Rome to Paris, and finally captured and imprisoned him in an effort to change his mind. Eventually, after two years of useless effort on the part of his mother and brothers, his sisters helped him escape.

He was taken by the Dominicans to Cologne to study under St. Albert the Great.[156] At the age of twenty-three, he was assigned as assistant professor to Albert. After four years in Cologne, he was sent back to Paris.

---

[155] Vaughan, *Life and Labours of St. Thomas*, 27.

[156] Saint Albertus Magnus (1200–1280).

Thomas was ordained a priest and continued to teach. He wrote books, several at a time. His *Summa Theologica* is an unmatched masterpiece of brilliant theology and spirituality. He also had a deep love for Our Lord in the Blessed Sacrament and wrote some of the most treasured hymns of the Church. He died at the age of forty-nine, in Fossanova, and is buried in Toulouse, France.

The word "ox" makes one think of a very large, slow-moving, slow-thinking, and stubborn animal that is fearsome because of its size, not necessarily for its ferocity. When provoked, an ox has a frightfully loud bellow. Slow to anger, it inspires terror when it finally reaches its limit of aggravation.

Saint Thomas Aquinas was a large man who was slow to speech and slow to anger, and many thought that he was stupid. He was probably Phlegmatic, and sometimes Phlegmatics are mistaken for being mentally slow because they do not put themselves forward like Cholerics and Sanguines. His fellow students in the class of Saint Albert the Great called him "the great, dumb, Sicilian ox."[157] One day, when he was being ridiculed, his illustrious teacher told the others, "We call this young man a dumb ox, but so loud will be his bellowing in doctrine that it will resound throughout the whole world."[158]

Imagine if those same condescending fellow students could know that when Pope St. Pius V

> ***Tip for Other Temperaments:***
> *Never underestimate the Phlegmatics in your life. Just because they are quiet, does not mean they are stupid.*

[157] Vaughan, *Life and Labours of St. Thomas*, 99.
[158] Vaughan, 103.

convoked the Council of Trent three hundred years later, he placed just two books on the altar as the guides for the Council! Those two books were the Holy Bible and the writings of the "dumb ox," St. Thomas Aquinas.

"His massive head betokened strength," wrote Archbishop Vaughan, referring to Thomas's physical appearance. "His broad tranquil brow, his placid meditative eyes, produced the impression, not so much of quickness and vivacity, as of breadth and command."[159]

The words the archbishop uses are strong indicators of temperament. If Thomas were Sanguine, we would see quickness and vivacity in his eyes. Placid and meditative, or peace-loving and thoughtful, are some adjectives often applied to a virtuous Phlegmatic.

Phlegmatics are naturally inclined to obstinacy but flee from conflict. This stubbornness can be set for something good, or for something bad. In Saint Thomas's case, he got it into his head to join the new order of Friars Preachers (Dominicans), begun by St. Dominic in 1216. His family rejected his decision unequivocally. They did not mind him having a religious vocation, but they wanted him to join a "respectable" preexisting order that would not disgrace the family name. In an effort to change his mind, they locked up the big, stubborn, slow-talking Thomas, in a tower in the family castle. But the more Choleric family members were being outwaited by the patient Phlegmatic. They wanted immediate results, as most Cholerics do, and they wanted their own way, as all Cholerics do. The more resistance Cholerics encounter, the more belligerent they become, until

[159] Vaughan, 19.

and unless they finally decide that the other person really is as tough as they are, and will not give way. It is at that moment that the Choleric's respect is won.

But before Thomas earned his family's respect, their belligerence toward his choice of life drove them to an imprudent plan. In desperation, they sent a prostitute into his tower room to distract him from his annoying desire to be a Dominican. At that moment, the long-suffering patience of the Phlegmatic ox was pushed to its limit. He seized a burning log from the great fireplace and drove the woman out. When he was being persecuted, he was meek and offered the persecution up as a sacrifice. But when temptation loomed, he became an angry bull.

Tip for Phlegmatics: *You may not talk as much as the other temperaments, and that's okay. Be sure that when you do speak, it is worthwhile.*

When Thomas was a child, being reared and educated as a Benedictine, it seemed that he fit right in with the monastic lifestyle—calm, quiet, thoughtful, prayerful. "Though he seldom spoke," wrote Archbishop Vaughan, "When he did speak, he set hearts beating faster."[160] Oftentimes, Phlegmatics will be "watchers"—silently watching the more active speakers in the room, but when they do speak, they are often witty and insightful.

Most Phlegmatics do not have to battle their passions of anger, impatience, and dramatic, tempestuous sorrow or frustration like Cholerics and Sanguines. They are born calmer and more laid-back. If Thomas was told to be silent in the corridors of the Abbey, it would have come easily to him.

---

[160] Vaughan, 19.

"The [Benedictine] Rule lays great stress on prayer," writes Archbishop Vaughan, himself a member of this order. "Thomas spent hours together, as a child, in meditation, so that all 'wondered at his power and his holiness.' . . . The Rule prescribes solitude: Thomas loved nothing better than to be alone."[161]

> ***Tip for Phlegmatics:*** *Use your time of silence to think, pray, and meditate.*

The monks taught Thomas religion, philosophy, and many other subjects, but they did not encourage intellectual pride, constant debating, or displays of competitive speech-making. This, again, fit right in with Thomas's temperament.

For those first seven years in the Abbey, Thomas thrived on the peace, silence, and abundant prayer time of the historic, holy monastery on the Italian hilltop. He thought, prayed, meditated, studied, learned, and obeyed the rules. Unlike a Choleric, he was not inclined to buck authority. Unlike a Sanguine, he was not tempted to run giggling through the hallways or incite the other boys to mischief. On the contrary, he encouraged the other boys to be good, and he had no desire to break the rules.

The Benedictines helped young Thomas learn how to combine activity with peace and tranquility. Tranquility does not have to mean idleness, nor does activity have to mean chaos or disturbance of mind.

His natural temperament was nourished and expanded by the life of grace in his soul. "He possessed that rare class of spiritual beauty which tells of gentleness, purity, and power," wrote Archbishop Vaughan.[162]

---

[161] Vaughan, 18.

[162] Vaughan, 19.

"There are many subtle influences which thrill to the inmost sanctuary of a sensitive spirit, which the less delicately strung have not the capacity to feel," wrote the archbishop.[163] Here he aptly describes the soul of a Phlegmatic or a Melancholic, of which Thomas was probably a combination. Thomas felt more deeply than others who did not share his temperament.

Tip for Phlegmatics: *You may think and feel things in a deeper way than those around you. Journal those thoughts and take them to God in prayer. You have great depth in your spirit.*

Cholerics and Sanguines may feel passionately, but they also change their moods and feelings often. Melancholics and Phlegmatics feel more on the inside. They do not necessarily wear their emotions on their sleeves, but often experience feelings and reactions that others may not even notice.

As a Phlegmatic, Thomas also possessed a strong will. Many Phlegmatics are accused of stubbornness or obstinacy. They will not openly fight, but they will quietly resist—to the end. The Benedictine Archbishop Vaughan beautifully describes Thomas's early life, "To breathe at peace under the light of truth, far from the contention of tongues, and then to meditate and resolve in the presence of one Eternal Witness—this has been the education of many a man of iron will, of soaring spirit, and of blameless life."[164]

Many Phlegmatics are born with an iron will and seem to be somewhat blameless because they never fight or scream or jump up and down in a tantrum. But that does not always mean they have a "soaring spirit." They may be inclined

---

[163] Vaughan, 18.

[164] Vaughan, 21.

to flop on the sofa and spend hours mindlessly watching television.

Thomas was not allowed to be lazy; he was encouraged to do his lessons and help in whatever way the monks needed. Diligence, performed peacefully, helped him to have clarity of vision and a strongly developed intellect. "From the center of stability, where rest alone is found, springs the activity of the thoughtful mind," wrote Archbishop Vaughan.[165] Other temperaments can learn stability and peacefulness from the Phlegmatics in their lives.

> ***Tip for Phlegmatics and Parents of Phlegmatic Children:***
> *Fill the mind with truth, beauty, and goodness. Encourage your peaceful spirit to soar, not just to flop on the ground in sloth.*

This may sound like a defense of Phlegmatics. It is true that stronger temperaments may disdain the peaceful Phlegmatic, thinking them worthless doormats. A virtuous Phlegmatic is hardworking, nonconfrontational, and meditative. A Phlegmatic who is not trying may be slothful and stubborn, like an old ox. But every temperament has its strengths, bestowed by God as gifts to help them on the way to salvation, and St. Thomas is a beautiful example of what a Phlegmatic, with some Melancholic, can become.

His mother Theodora and his two older brothers sound like they were Choleric. When Thomas was forced to leave Monte Cassino, where he would be trained by the Benedictines from age five to twelve, he came back to his family. His mother was still insistent that he be groomed to become Abbot of Monte Cassino someday. Her older sons were fighters, and she could see Thomas was not cut out to be a soldier. Since he was drawn to the religious life, she felt he could

[165] Vaughan, 22.

give honor to the family and strengthen their political and military position by becoming the powerful Abbot of the most important monastery in Italy. Cholerics are often filled with ambition, which can be unfathomable to a Phlegmatic.

She sent Thomas to Naples, a city of great learning at the time. There were two Benedictine monasteries there that were related to Monte Cassino. He probably lived in one of them as he attended university. But in this city, he came in contact with the Dominicans.

"The special scope of the [Dominican] order, its love for learning, its active ministrations to humanity while still retaining the self-restraint of solitaries and the humility of monks, must have struck a new chord, or an old chord in a new fashion, in the heart of the Saint," wrote Archbishop Vaughan.[166]

It made perfect sense that an intellectual like Thomas would be drawn to this order of those who studied and preached. Archbishop Vaughan tells us, "To the stability, largeness, and self-control of the Benedictine he was going to add the learning, eloquence, and judicial steadiness of a Dominican."[167]

A huge crowd gathered to watch the promising young student Thomas join the Dominican Order. As soon as his mother heard about it, she rushed to Naples to complain. Archbishop Vaughan says, "Theodora had already made up her mind about the will of God in her son's regard."[168] What a great description of a Choleric! Cholerics often think they

---

[166] Vaughan, 46.
[167] Vaughan, 47.
[168] Vaughan, 69.

know the will of God for others, but that can only be learned by prayer, meditation, and spiritual guidance.

When the Dominicans found out she was coming, they bundled the new novice off to Rome, avoiding the main roads. Theodora must have had the quite reputation for forcefulness and getting her own way. When she reached Naples and found they had gone to Rome, she chased angrily after him.

Tip for All Temperaments: *Seek the will of God by prayer, meditation, and spiritual direction.*

Theodora stormed and raged at the gates of the Santa Sabina convent in Rome, but the Dominicans would not admit her. Next, Thomas fled to Paris with some of his new religious confreres. When Theodora figured out where he was going, she sent a messenger to her two soldier sons telling them to intercept Thomas.

His brothers Landulf and Reginald literally captured him with an armed band of soldiers and carried him off to the family home in San Giovanni. Thankfully, it is not legal nowadays for older Choleric brothers to force a young adult to give up the state of life he has chosen.

His fiery Italian mother stormed at Thomas and pleaded with him. She tried everything she could think of to change his mind, but he remained quietly determined. Finally, she locked him up and set guards to watch his prison, hoping to overcome his obstinacy.

His mother and older brothers had tried to force their will on him; next, his sisters tried to cajole him into surrender. "But the calm deportment of the future Angel of the Schools, his resignation, his tenderness to his sisters, his tranquil mind ever fixed on things Divine, were more powerful, in the end, than creature stubbornness, or human passion," wrote Archbishop Vaughan.[169] Thomas, who would later be named patron saint of Catholic Schools, converted his sisters to his cause.

At this time, Thomas's wild brothers sent the young woman in to try to seduce their brother, and he drove her out with a burning stick from the fireplace. When he had done this, Thomas threw himself on his knees and made a vow of chastity. Our Lord blessed him with a vision, in which angels tied a girdle of purity around him. From then on, he was never tempted against holy purity. This freedom helped his intellect to flourish even more.

> ***Tip for Phlegmatics:***
> *You have a huge capacity for quiet determination and immovability, which can be a help to your virtue. Make sure that what you choose to be stubborn about is listening, following, and obeying the will of God—and then stand strong.*

Thomas's sisters told the Dominicans about their brother's two-year imprisonment. His fellow monks appealed to the pope, who put pressure on the emperor to make his soldiers Landulf and Reginald release Thomas. They still would not do it, so finally, the girls lowered their brother out a window and helped him to escape with his brother Dominicans.

The Dominicans knew that Thomas had great potential, so they wanted to entrust his formation and education to the greatest Dominican teacher they knew—St. Albert the Great. As they approached Paris before heading to Cologne to find Albert, the Dominican superior asked Thomas, "What would you give, Brother Thomas, to be king of that city?"

Thomas, a bookish, intellectual Phlegmatic, responded, "I would rather have St. John Chrysostom's treatise on the

[169] Vaughan, 75.

Gospel of St. Matthew, than be king of the whole of France."[170] Some people try to tell us that we must all have ambition for this world's glories, but Thomas gives us an example of a great saint who wanted none of it. He was happy with a book written by another saint.

At Cologne, as a student under St. Albert the Great, Thomas's classmates referred to him as "the dumb ox." We may wonder why a man with such a prodigious intellect (and prodigious physical size, so they say) would be silent in class, despite being taunted.

> ***Tip for Sanguines, Cholerics, and Melancholics:*** *Learn from the silence and restraint of Phlegmatics.*

Archbishop Vaughan suggests that Thomas might have been intimidated by Albertus Magnus (Albert the Great) and so he wanted to just listen and learn. He also says the deep thoughts that Thomas was experiencing inclined him to silence and contemplation, and that "he may have felt, in his extreme modesty, that his mind had not arrived at that maturity which makes the ventilation of difficult problems of much advantage; and that now was the time to listen and learn, not to talk and teach: and that truth is arrived at by slow degrees, through patient, unwearied thought, and through the laborious comparison of a thousand experiences."[171]

When we imagine a Choleric young adult in this same position, the difference is almost laughable. What Choleric teen or young adult would decide that he should just listen and learn? Would they think they should not ventilate their every thought or opinion? In this, they can learn from the

[170] Vaughan, 85.
[171] Vaughan, 97.

Phlegmatics. Likewise, a Sanguine likes to be the center of attention. Sanguines sometimes struggle to apply themselves to "patient, unwearied thought." St. Thomas was definitely not a Sanguine. While he knew more than all the other students in the room, he kept his peace.

This saint's Phlegmatic temperament was a great tool in his mission in this world—to penetrate some of the deep mysteries of the Faith. This could only be done by someone with a great mind, who had no intellectual pride in his own abilities. It needed to be someone, also, who spent time in deep thinking and prayer, and did not just jump to random conclusions, depending on his own mental prowess.

> ***Tip for Phlegmatics:***
> *If you are ridiculed, remember how little others' opinions matter. Focus on pleasing God.*

Each one of us has been given a mission by God. We may not know what it is at this time of our lives, but if we pray, are open to His will, and use the talents He gave us, we will be ready for it.

Archbishop Vaughan speculates, "He must often silently have smiled at their blunders whilst they were thinking to dazzle him by their talent and acuteness."[172] It honestly did not matter to Thomas to have to prove his intelligence.

We are told that the saint was not only silent in the classroom, but also at recreation. "That they all taunted him publicly, and called by his nicknames to his face, is evident from the surest testimony. But the Saint had been well broken to suffering, and he bore it all without a word. And being a

---

[172] Vaughan, 100.

youth of real breadth of mind, he knew how much all this was worth, and took it at its proper valuation."[173]

Phlegmatics who may be bullied or ridiculed can take their cue from this saint. He knew how little his classmates' opinions and thoughts mattered, and his only concern was to know, love, and serve God. The more they left him alone, the more time he had to pray and think.

Some Phlegmatics might be told, "You should stand up for yourself. Why don't you tell that person off?" But if you do not want to engage in conflict, do not do it. There are times when we must stand up for the honor or glory of God, or for the Truth, but if we do not want to engage in pointless conflict, there is no obligation. As a matter of fact, there is more merit in keeping our peace. As the saying goes, "You don't have to attend every argument you're invited to." Most Phlegmatics take this to heart.

Eventually, the world, including his peers and classmates, felt the influence of his great mind. Phlegmatics often take time to make their mark on the world. He was in no rush. He spent his time contemplating the Infinite.

As his career progressed, he would sometimes debate, but he still never lost his cool. He disputed issues calmly and with great charity. In his entire life, he was not known to lose his temper. Part of that came from his temperament, but he also practiced great virtue by the grace of God.

"His humility and sweetness came out strikingly when arguing in the schools," Archbishop Vaughan tells us. "He

---

[173] Vaughan, 99.

answered meekly, and with benevolence—steadied by the light from which his every action sprang."[174]

He became an assistant professor to Albert and was ordained a priest. His life was full of thought, prayer, study, and work. After offering Holy Mass, and giving his lectures in school, he would dictate to three or four secretaries at once, on different subjects. The rest of his day was spent in prayer and more writing.

"He was like the lighthouse, in a noisy, washing sea—calm and steady—and, in the midst of the whirling and seething, the rising and breaking, the lashing and sinking of the objectless waters—ever biding in one place, ever consistently fulfilling one appointed mission, ever throwing the light that was in him upon the instability of all around," wrote Archbishop Vaughan.[175]

Tip for Phlegmatics: *Cultivate your devotion to Our Lord in the Blessed Sacrament by frequent attendance at daily Mass. His peaceful patience in the Eucharist will bring light to your soul and draw you closer to His Heart.*

He prayed at his Mass each day for the conversion of his brothers, the ones who had captured and imprisoned him. They eventually saw the error of their ways and left the emperor's cause and espoused the pope's instead. The emperor stormed their castle at Aquino, and they died in the battle. St. Thomas was consoled by a message from Heaven that his brothers' souls were saved.

Some people mistakenly accuse Phlegmatics of not having feelings. But Thomas showed his deep capacity for love, not only in his forgiveness of his brothers, but in his devotion

[174] Vaughan, 175.
[175] Vaughan, 100.

to Our Lord in the Blessed Sacrament. Pope Urban IV, recognizing his great talent, asked him to write the Mass and Office for the Feast of Corpus Christi.

When we attend Benediction of the Blessed Sacrament, we also sing the hymns written by this great saint: *Tantum Ergo, O Salutaris Hostia*, as well as *Panis Angelicus, Adoro Te Devote*, and *Lauda Sion*.

One of the biggest obstructions to the spiritual life of a Phlegmatic is a lack of industriousness. St. Jerome[176] tells us that it is better to keep busy, so that when temptation comes, you are occupied. A Phlegmatic would often rather lie around watching television or sleeping, vaguely hoping that someone else will do the work. They do not actually refuse to do it; they just procrastinate—mightily.

But this great weakness of laziness was not an issue for St. Thomas Aquinas. He worked tirelessly to use the talents God gave him, peacefully and diligently, until his early death at the age of forty-nine.

Tip for Phlegmatics: *Imitate the work ethic of St. Thomas Aquinas. Keep busy with God's work.*

About one year before his death, one of the other monks hid in the church of San Domenico at Naples to watch the great Thomas pray. Fra Domenico di Caserta saw Thomas lifted in the air, as he prayed before an icon of the Crucifixion.

"Whilst the Saint was thus entranced, Fra Domenico distinctly heard Christ's voice saying from the image: 'Well hast thou written of Me, Thomas. What reward wilt thou accept for thy labour?'"[177]

---

[176] Saint Jerome (c. 342–420).

[177] Vaughan, 378–379.

St. Thomas had definitely reached the pinnacle of success as a writer.

How did this thoughtful, prayerful saint respond?

"No other than Thyself, O Lord!"[178]

He had narrowed his focus, like St. Mary Magdalene did in her way, to the best part, the only thing that matters—our relationship with Christ.

[178] Vaughan, 379.

8

Another Phlegmatic Thomas—Married with Children

Phlegmatic

Saint Thomas More was born on February 7, 1478, in London, and was the second of six children. His father was a lawyer who became a judge. He decided that Thomas would follow in his footsteps. The boy attended St. Anthony's School on Threadneedle Street, and then at the age of thirteen, was sent to be a page in Cardinal Morton's household at Lambeth Palace.

In 1492, Thomas went to Canterbury College, Oxford, for his continued education. After two years, he went back to London to further study law at Lincoln's Inn. He loved to pray and read, and he often did physical penance, like wearing a hairshirt.

Thomas entered the London Charterhouse, a strict monastery, and stayed there for four years, fasting, praying, and discerning his vocation. At the end of that time, he decided that God was calling him to the lay state.

We are told by his son-in-law Will Roper, as quoted by Rt. Rev. Mgr. Hallett, that when he was about twenty-seven, Thomas went to see Mr. Colt in Essex, who had "three daughters whose honest conversation and virtuous education provoked him there especially to set his affection." Roper also tells us that Thomas liked the second daughter best, but "when he considered that it would be both great grief and some shame also to the eldest to see her younger sister in marriage preferred before her, he then of a certain pity framed his fancy towards her and soon after married her."[179]

Thomas and Jane were very happy, and they were blessed with four children—Margaret, Elizabeth, Cecily, and John, but when Margaret was only six, Thomas's dear wife died. About a month later, he asked his priest for a dispensation to marry again right away, not so much for love this time, but for the practicality of a mother for his children. His second wife, Alice, was a widow with a daughter. He also adopted a girl named Margaret Giggs, who later married one of his children's tutors. Thomas could be called a "homeschool dad" in that he was a pioneer in educating his daughters as well as his son.

He was a successful lawyer, was knighted, and even rose to be Speaker of the House of Commons. After the death of Cardinal Wolsey, he was appointed Lord Chancellor of England, a position second only to the king. The king leaned on him as a friend and counselor.

After two and a half years in this position, he resigned in 1532, claiming ill health. But Thomas was seeing the ill winds of King Henry VIII's passions blowing through the court and the kingdom. Wanting to avoid the conflict, he stepped down.

For a short time, he experienced peace at home with his children, their spouses, and his eleven grandchildren. He

---

[179] Hallett, *Saint Thomas More*, 3.

had time to pray, think, teach his children, and enjoy family time. But then, as he expected, Henry VIII decided to put aside his wife Catherine and enter an adulterous liaison with Anne Boleyn, (whom he later ordered to be beheaded). Since the Catholic Church does not permit divorce, Henry declared himself the head of the Church in England and broke away from the Faith.

The king demanded that Thomas agree to his sins. He ordered the clergy and nobles, including Thomas, to sign the Act of Supremacy, which declared Henry the "pope" of England, independent of Rome. When Thomas refused, he was imprisoned in the Bell Tower, part of the Tower of London.

He stayed in prison for fifteen months, until they took him out on July 1, 1535, to "try him for treason" at Westminster Hall, where a plaque still marks the spot. As a lawyer, he defended himself, saying that he had only kept silent; he had never spoken against the king or his choices. But like Our Lord, Thomas was betrayed by a false witness. A man named Richard Rich claimed that Thomas had said treasonous things.

Monsignor Hallett quotes the saint as saying in court, "If this oath of yours, Mr. Rich, be true, then pray I that I may never see God in the face, which I would not say, were it otherwise, to win the whole world. . . . In faith, Mr. Rich, I am sorrier for your perjury than for mine own peril."[180]

But the judges were determined to find him guilty, since that would please the king. When they condemned him to death, Monsignor Hallett says the saint responded, "As the

[180] Hallett, 24.

blessed Apostle St. Paul was present and consented to the death of St. Stephen, and yet be they now both twain holy saints in Heaven, so I verily trust and shall therefore right heartily pray, that though your Lordships have now in earth been judges to my condemnation, we may yet hereafter in Heaven merrily all meet together to our everlasting salvation."[181]

On Tuesday, July 6, 1535, St. Thomas More was beheaded. His beloved daughter Margaret rescued his head and buried it in the Roper Family Vault in Canterbury. He was beatified in 1886 and canonized in 1935.

Teresa Lloyd, in her booklet *A Child's Life of Blessed Thomas More*, records that when he was a baby, Thomas was being carried by a nurse on horseback. As the nurse crossed a river, the horse stumbled in the current, and the nurse feared for the baby. She threw him over a hedge onto the riverbank for safety.

When she made it to land, she found him calm and smiling.[182] Calm and smiling—there you have a description of most Phlegmatics, and St. Thomas More gives us a superb example of a Phlegmatic saint.

He is especially remembered for his peacefulness amid a tempestuous time in England, as well as his wit and joviality. He does not seem to have been a noisy man, wanting to be the life of every party like a Sanguine.

Phlegmatic humor is clever and witty, but it is delivered in a quiet way, with a twinkle in the eye. Often, people do not

---

[181] Hallett, 24–25.

[182] Lloyd, *Child's Life of Blessed Thomas More*, 3.

even realize that the Phlegmatic was paying attention until they throw out the perfect line of wit, quietly, during a lull in the noise. You will not find a Phlegmatic climbing on a chair, yelling, "Hey everybody! Over here! You've got to hear this great joke I just came up with!"

"The wit and humor of the Saints is very instructive," wrote Fr. Aloysius Roche. "It reminds us of what we are apt to forget, of what we sometimes do not even suspect, that there is more real joy in a Saint's life than there is in all the intoxication of worldliness. All that comes from God is joyous and holiness comes straight from Him."[183]

St. Thomas More gives us a good example of this. "A man can live for the next world but be merry withal,"[184] he often said. He even joked when he knew that he was probably going to lose his life. The Duke of Norfolk advised him that he should not disagree with the king, quoting, "The anger of a prince is death." Thomas replied, "Then the only difference between us is that I shall die today, and you will die tomorrow."[185]

He often told his children, "A man may very well lose his head, yet come to no harm."[186] His clear-sightedness and perceptive legal mind foresaw that he might very well be beheaded for principle, but he still made quips about it.

After being repeatedly pestered by messengers and noblemen and henchmen of Henry VIII to change his mind about taking the heretical Oath of Supremacy, Thomas finally sent

---

[183] Roche, *A Bedside Book of Saints*, 75.
[184] Lloyd, *Child's Life of Blessed Thomas More*, 5.
[185] As quoted in Hallett, *Saint Thomas More*, 14.
[186] Hallett, 15.

word through the latest messenger that he had changed his mind. When the excited messenger returned from the king to get more details, Thomas must have had a twinkle in his eye. He told the messenger that he had changed his mind about being shaved, that he would be executed with a beard instead!

As he climbed the scaffold, he asked the Lieutenant to help him up the stairs, but said, "At my coming down, let me shift for myself." His last audible words were another joke. As he lay his head on the block, he said, "One moment, let me move my beard. Pity that should be cut: that has not committed treason."[187]

> ***Tip for Phlegmatics:*** *You have probably been blessed with a good sense of humor. Use it to lighten others' load and to spread good cheer.*

As he became more successful, his wit and humor were even desired at court. The only way that Thomas could get King Henry VIII to let him go home, writes Mgr. Hallett, was "to pretend to have lost his merriment, and the king would good-naturedly take the hint and allow him leave of absence"[188] to go home to his family. Sometimes the king would drop by unannounced at the More family home in Chelsea.

The king continued to promote Thomas higher and higher in politics and law, but Thomas remained untouched by all the worldly glamor. He stayed impartial and fair when put in a position to judge. One time, his own wife had acquired a sweet little dog that she loved, and then a poor woman came forward and claimed it was hers. To be totally fair, Thomas told his wife and the poor woman to go to opposite ends of the hall and call the dog. When the dog ran to the

---

[187] Hallett, 27.

[188] Hallett, 6.

poor lady, Thomas decreed that the dog was hers. Alice More worked it out—she bought the dog from the poor woman for an exorbitant price.

Like St. Thomas Aquinas, this Thomas was clear-sighted and intelligent. He was pious and recollected, and enjoyed prayer and meditation regularly, which deepened his spirituality.

His second wife was good at household finance, which worked well because Thomas was very open-handed. Alice was loving to all their children. Mgr. Hallett writes, "No one could well get cross with so cheerful a husband as Thomas More. Between them there was constant good-humored jesting."[189]

> ***Tip for Phlegmatics:*** *Your peacefulness will be an asset in marriage and business. Treasure that calmness and good temper.*

In Old Chelsea Church, visitors can still read the epitaph written by St. Thomas More for his first wife, expressing the hope that he and his second wife would both be buried there together someday. Instead of setting them against each other, or comparing one negatively to the other, he wished that they could both be friends in Heaven.

He was a peacemaker in his law practice as well as at home. He tried to get the litigants to settle out of court whenever possible.

Thomas kindly and peacefully corrected his children. Mgr. Hallett writes, "When correction was required, he gave it so gently that Margaret Giggs in later years used to relate that sometimes she deliberately committed some trifling fault,

[189] Hallett, 4.

so sweet and loving was his reproof."[190] Roper, his son-in-law, lived in the same house with him for sixteen years and declares that he never saw Thomas angry.

He tried to keep the peace even when he could see the dark clouds gathering. He stepped down from his illustrious position of wealth and influence to try to avoid the clash he knew would come with King Henry VIII. This made him much poorer, but he happily made the best of it, encouraging his family to do the same.

When confronted with the Oath of Supremacy that he could not take, he again tried to keep the peace. "He expressed his willingness to swear to the succession as fixed by King and Parliament," wrote Mgr. Hallett. This meant that he was willing to swear that Henry could decree that the children of Anne Boleyn could succeed to the throne. "But to the oath in the form in which it was presented to him, implying a denial of the authority of the Pope, he said he could not swear 'without the jeoparding of his soul to perpetual damnation,' and from that position, despite their most earnest argument and persuasion, he refused to budge."[191]

Thomas would not swear to the Oath of Supremacy, but he would not enter into a debate over why, because he knew they would use that as an excuse to kill him. He used that holy Phlegmatic stubbornness, like Thomas Aquinas, to quietly stick to God's will no matter what.

To his wife, children, and grandchildren, Thomas More was a beautiful example of prayer, meditation, and talking about spiritual things. He served Mass in Old Chelsea

---

190 Hallett, 9.

191 Hallett, 18.

Church near their home, where he endowed a wing that can still be visited. One of the priests who served that parish was afterwards martyred, Blessed John Larke. Teresa Lloyd points out, "One future martyr served the Mass of another."[192]

He would also put on a surplice and sing in the choir, even at the height of his career. He carried the cross during the Rogation Days processions. Phlegmatics have more of a normal tendency to humility than other temperaments, but Thomas also worked hard to be virtuous.

Mgr. Hallett quotes him as telling his children, "It is now no mastery for you children to go to Heaven for everybody giveth you good example. But if you live in the time that no man will give you good counsel, nor no man will give you good example, when you shall see virtue punished and vice rewarded, if you will then stand fast and firmly stick to God upon pain of life, if you be but half good, God will allow you for whole good."[193]

He knew that the good days of peace would not last. When he first retired, he said that now he could "bestow the residue of my life to come about the provision for my soul in the service of God."[194] He prayed, read, and wrote—a beautiful balance of peaceful time with intellectual work.

Thomas wrote to his friend Erasmus that he was now blessedly freed from "the troublesome business of public affairs" and could now "live some while only to God and myself."[195] He also began telling stories of the martyrs to his children, perhaps foreseeing his own martyrdom. Teresa Lloyd writes

---

[192] Lloyd, *Child's Life of Blessed Thomas More*, 9.

[193] Hallett, *Saint Thomas More*, 8.

[194] Hallett, 14.

[195] As quoted in Lloyd, *Child's Life of Blessed Thomas More*, 10.

that St. Thomas told his family "how great a comfort it would be to him if his wife and children were actually to encourage him to die in a good cause, 'for it would cause him for joy thereof merrily to run to death.'"[196]

On May 4, 1535, his daughter Margaret was visiting him in prison as the first martyrs of King Henry VIII's reign were taken to Tyburn to be executed. Thomas and Margaret were looking out the Bell Tower window and saw them. "Lo, dost thou not see, Meg, that those blessed fathers be now as cheerfully going to their deaths as bridegrooms to their marriage?"[197] Then he advised her that he himself was not nearly worthy of such a blessing, and he berated himself for his worldliness. Once again, he was teaching his daughter.

In his last letter to her, he wrote, "Farewell, my dear child, and pray for me, and I shall for you and all your friends, that we may merrily meet in Heaven."[198] He sent her his hairshirt as a remembrance. It reminds us of Blessed Margaret Clitherow,[199] who sent her daughter Anne her stockings from prison before her martyrdom, to remind Anne to walk in her footsteps.

When the messenger brought Thomas word that it was time to be executed, the messenger wept. The saint, who knew he was going to see God that day, said cheerfully, "I trust we shall once in Heaven see each other full merrily,

---

[196] Lloyd, 11.

[197] As quoted in Lloyd, 12.

[198] As quoted in Hallett, *Saint Thomas More*, 25–26.

[199] Blessed Margaret Clitherow (1556–1586).

where we shall be sure to live and love together in joyful bliss eternally."[200]

As he walked up the hill from the Tower of London to the scaffold (now marked with a stone tablet that can still be seen), he encountered a man that had been struggling with thoughts of discouragement and despair.

"Do you know me, Sir Thomas?" called out the man. "I pray you, for Our Lord's sake to help me: I am as ill troubled as ever I was."

But the saint replied calmly, "I remember thee full well. Go thy ways in peace and pray for me: and I will not fail to pray for thee."[201] From that moment, the man was healed from his despondency and never suffered from temptations to despair again.

> ***Tip for all Temperaments:*** *Take the opportunities God gives you to encourage others. It is a great act of charity to lift others' spirits, even when you are suffering.*

When Thomas first entered prison, he was still able to read and write, but eventually, the king, to punish him further, ordered that all his papers and books be removed from his cell. He still managed a couple of times to write a letter to his daughter Margaret with a piece of charcoal.

His wife Alice visited and tried to convince him to sign the oath, as had so many clerics of his time. She urged him to succumb so that he could come home to them at Chelsea and be happy again.

"How long then, Mistress Alice, do you think I may enjoy a happy life at Chelsea?" he asked, probably with a kindly twinkle.

---

[200] Lloyd, *Child's Life of Blessed Thomas More*, 14.
[201] Hallett, *Saint Thomas More*, 26.

"A full twenty years," she said. "You are not old yet."

"My good wife," said the saintly lawyer, "You are not very skillful at a bargain. Would you have me, for twenty years, give up eternity?"[202]

Virtuous Phlegmatics like Thomas More are also diligent "worker bees." They are often not distracted by ambition or avarice. They do have to watch out for sloth, but Thomas More gives us a wonderful example of his work ethic. When he was Chancellor, he caught up on all the outstanding cases, which was unheard of at the time.

Even the man who ordered his death, the adulterous King Henry VIII, loved and respected Thomas. "It is recorded," writes Mgr. Hallett, "That when news was brought of the execution, the king rose from the table where he had been playing dice with Anne Boleyn, accused her of being the cause of More's death, and left the room shedding bitter tears."[203]

God knows exactly when and where to place each of us. Saint Thomas More spent four years in a monastery. Think of how different his story would have been if he had become a monk instead of a husband, father, and Lord Chancellor of England! We would have been deprived of his wonderful example to laypeople. God knew the specific time and place where Thomas More would shine. If we are in the place where God wants us to be, wonderful things happen.

Tip to Phlegmatics: *Be a diligent worker-bee like St. Thomas. Don't be discouraged by the politics that swirls around you—in your family, office, or country—but faithfully perform the duties of your state in life.*

[202] Hallett, 19.
[203] Hallett, 27.

God's watch is not broken. He has not forgotten about the world today. He planted us right here in the middle of the battlefield because He knows that this is the perfect place for us to shine. We are following in the footsteps of the saints. Let us follow their examples, peacefully doing our duty with a good sense of humor, like St. Thomas. As he said, "Pray for me, and I will pray for you, that we may merrily meet in Heaven!"[204]

---

[204] Hallett, 25–26.

9

Was St. Joseph a Phlegmatic?

Phlegmatic-Melancholic

St. Matthew (chapter 1) and St. Luke (chapter 3) record different fathers for St. Joseph, so St. Augustine tells us St. Joseph was probably adopted.[205] He probably had a brother named Cleophas, because Mary of Cleophas was referred to as Our Lady's sister. Since St. Anne and St. Joachim, the parents of the Blessed Virgin, had no other children, it seems likely that Mary, wife of Cleophas, was Our Lady's sister-in-law.

When Our Lady was fourteen, she was still living in the Temple with the other young, consecrated maidens, and her parents had passed away. It fell to the high priest to find her a suitable husband. As each Jewish man or woman married members of their own tribe, he chose one from the tribe of David, little knowing that he was fulfilling the age-old prophecy that the Savior would be born from the house and lineage of David. St. Joseph was miraculously chosen to be the pure spouse of the Virgin Mary.

[205] Levy, *Joseph the Just Man*, 12–13.

We know some of the major scenes of his life from Scripture, and since he was absent from his holy spouse's side at Calvary, we have always believed that Joseph had previously died in the arms of Jesus and Mary. Because of this, he is the patron saint of a happy death.

Saint Joseph appears in many key scenes in the Bible, but his words are never recorded. His sweet spouse, gentlest and humblest of all women, speaks, but he never does. We hear from the Choleric St. Paul, the Sanguine St. Peter, the Melancholic-Sanguine St. Mary Magdalene, and the Melancholic St. John. However, we never hear any words of St. Joseph.

This may be because he was Phlegmatic. He did not need many words; he was a man of quiet, peaceful action. He had no need to make himself heard. Even if we cannot confirm whether or not St. Joseph was a Phlegmatic, we can learn much from this faithful husband and father.

He loved, he worked, he moved things along, but he did so silently and faithfully. Phlegmatics are often quiet and introverted, with no need to be the center of attention. Even without supernatural, acquired virtue, they have no desire to steal the spotlight or start a ruckus. They are, by nature, peace-loving, calm, and patient.

Without grace, they can become lazy and apathetic, and they can become likely to compromise their principles for the sake of keeping the peace. They want to avoid conflict at all costs. They are quietly strong-willed. They may not openly defy you, but once they dig their heels in, they will nod their heads, seeming to agree to avoid confrontation, and then do exactly what they like.

One of the first crises Joseph had to handle was the pregnancy of his lovely wife. They were betrothed—which was more than an engagement. They were, for all intents and purposes, married, but it was the custom of the time and place to have a lapse of time before they came to live in the same house. St. Joseph knew well that they had both taken vows of virginity.

Scripture tells us that the Incarnation of Our Lord Jesus Christ took place after their betrothal: "A virgin espoused to a man whose name was Joseph" (Luke 1:27) but "before they came together" (Matt. 1:18). Because they were not living in the same house yet, he had no knowledge of the powerful angel Gabriel's visit to the Blessed Virgin, bringing her the news that would save all mankind. Like all devout Jews, Joseph waited and prayed for the coming of the Messiah.

Joseph's sweet bride told him that her aging cousin Elizabeth was with child and humbly asked permission to wait upon her. God and the angels alone shared her secret that she was carrying the Maker of Heaven and earth beneath her joyful young heart. Joseph immediately agreed and even escorted her into the hill country to Zachary's house to ensure her safety. It was a sacrifice to be deprived of the consolation of her company, but he offered it peacefully, in submission to the law of charity.

It is likely that Joseph saw Mary safely into the care of her relative Zachary, who had been struck mute by the angel Gabriel for not believing his message about the birth of his son, John the Baptist. Joseph then headed back home to work for the support of his wife and their future home together. Since Joseph and Mary had each made a vow of virginity, he did not expect to have any children, but he still worked hard to provide a decent livelihood for the two of them.

He did not hear the exuberant Elizabeth when she said, "Blessed art thou among women, and blessed is the fruit of thy womb. And whence is this to me, that the *Mother of my Lord* should come to me?" (Luke 1:42–43, emphasis added).

Three or four months elapsed, and the gentle Virgin Mother was ready to go home to Nazareth and begin living with Joseph in their humble abode by his workshop. Imagine his astonishment and consternation when he arrived to pick her up, and he saw that his glowing fifteen-year-old wife was beginning to show! The Gospel of Luke tells us that he was understandably troubled.

A Choleric would have wanted to storm, "Look here, Mary, what's this all about?" But being Phlegmatic, and probably Melancholic too, St. Joseph was troubled. If he had been a rigorous man: a strong Melancholic-Choleric, he might have said, "I don't know what happened exactly, because I can't believe Mary would do anything wrong, but the law is clear. I have to expose her and condemn her." A Sanguine might have been inclined to be a liberal and say, "Oh, well, it doesn't matter. I'm not going to worry about it. It's great to see you again, Mary!"

Saint Joseph, being a virtuous man and probably a Phlegmatic-Melancholic, waited and prayed. He did not rush into any rash actions. Phlegmatics almost never rush into taking action. He waited and prayed for God to make His will known. He wondered where his moral responsibility lay, as the Mosaic Law was clear that no man could remain with an adulteress. He worried that she might be stoned for adultery when he knew in his heart that she was innocent. Truly, there was a mystery here that he did not understand.

The Blessed Virgin Mary was wise. She had seen his startled reaction, and knew he was struggling. She compassionated him, but we know from Holy Scripture that she did not reveal to him the truth about her precious cargo. It was not her place to spread the news. Elizabeth had been Divinely inspired to know the truth; Almighty God could easily enlighten her bewildered husband, if He so wished. In the meantime, she waited and prayed.

> ***Tip for Phlegmatics and All Temperaments:*** *When you are perplexed, take time to pray and make a prudent decision in tranquility, like St. Joseph.*

We too can act this way in our lives and follow the example of Mary and Joseph. Our heavenly Mother sees that we have a bewildering problem or a painful trial, but if God wishes us to suffer through it, then she stands at the foot of our cross patiently, supporting and compassionating us.

Joseph's patience in this trial was soon rewarded by a comforting and thrilling message from an angel. "Joseph, son of David, fear not to take unto thee Mary thy wife [under your roof], for that which is conceived in her, is of the Holy Ghost. And she shall bring forth a son: and thou shalt call His name JESUS. For He shall save His people from their sins" (Matt. 1:20–21).

Every time an angel comes to visit St. Joseph (which happens several times that we know of), he accepts the message and instructions without question. He does not express disbelief like Zachary, for which Elizabeth's husband was struck dumb. He does not even ask respectfully, "How shall this be done?" (Luke 1:34), like Our Lady did at the Annunciation. He accepts it simply and immediately. This is also very typical of a Phlegmatic person. They do not need to question or understand every bit of it, they accept events, messages, and changes more easily than other temperaments.

No doubt his heart was filled with relief and joy, perhaps mixed with some fear of the great mission with which he would been entrusted. The approved private revelations of Venerable Mary of Agreda tell us that St. Joseph was thirty-three years old when this happened.[206]

Rosalie Marie Levy says that he was the pinnacle of all the Old Testament heroes. "Like Abraham, Joseph was a man of faith and obedience; like Isaac, a man of prayer and vision; like Jacob, a man of patience and self-sacrifice; like Joseph of Egypt, a man of purity; like David, a man according to God's own Heart."[207]

Since God Himself was the Father of the child Jesus, we might wonder why Our Lady needed to marry at all. St. Jerome, as quoted by Rosalie Marie Levy, explains it this way: "Firstly, that by the genealogy of Joseph the lineage of Mary might be shown." Jewish genealogies were always listed by the male side, and it was known that if Joseph was of the tribe of David, then his wife was too. "Secondly,"

---

[206] According to the *Catholic Encyclopedia*, "When the Church approves private revelations, she declares only that there is nothing in them contrary faith or good morals, and that they may be read without danger or even with profit; no obligation is thereby imposed on the faithful to believe them."

[207] Levy, 27.

continues Levy, "Lest she should be stoned by the Jews as an adulteress. Thirdly, that she might have a comforter when fleeing into Egypt."[208]

What a tribute to St. Joseph, that he was chosen to be the comforter to the Blessed Mother and her precious child! God also knew that Joseph, with his balanced mind and peaceful obedience, would be able to handle the ups and downs of a life as the foster-father of the God-Man.

St. John Chrysostom tells us that when the angel told Joseph, "Thou shalt call His name JESUS" (Matt. 1:21), he was entrusting the earthly fatherhood of the child to Joseph. In the Jewish custom of the day, the father always declared the name of the child.[209] St. Luke refers to Mary and Joseph as "His parents" (Luke 2:27). In every way except begetting, Joseph was the father of Our Lord.

> ***Tip for Phlegmatics:*** *You have a balanced, calm personality—so God may entrust you with great missions for His Glory. Be not afraid; put all your trust in Him.*

St. Bernard of Clairvaux calls St. Joseph "a man after God's Own Heart."[210] That is good food for meditation—how can we imitate St. Joseph in being patient, obedient, and prudent?

The young married couple went along happily for several months, and the time for Christ's birth approached. Another challenge arose. This one was not from an angel, but from the government. They were forced to journey eighty-five miles in winter weather to Bethlehem to enroll in the census. The prophets had foretold that the Messiah would be born

---

[208] Levy, 33.
[209] Levy, 37.
[210] As quoted in Levy, 42.

in Bethlehem and the secular leader (Caesar) was unknowingly the tool of God's will.

> ***Tip for All Temperaments:*** *Sometimes, in spite of our best efforts, we do not succeed in what we set out to do for God. We can accept this humbly as His Divine will, like Mary and Joseph did.*

Joseph suffered greatly when his expectant wife had no place to lay her head. As a provider, Joseph wanted desperately to fulfill what he thought was his mission. But sometimes, no matter what we do, we do not succeed at what we attempt for the glory of God. Joseph probably apologized to Mary profusely when he found a dirty stable in a cave on a hillside as the only possible shelter. He probably felt like a failure as a husband and father. Regardless of how hard we try, sometimes we do not succeed in what we attempt for the glory of God. It is not His will.

Joseph was rewarded for his efforts when the shepherds and then the Wise Men came to adore his foster-son, the Son of God. His heart rejoiced to see that some recognized the Messiah who had come into the world. After forty days, the Christ child was presented, according to the Law, in the Temple in Jerusalem. Joseph again probably rejoiced when Anna and Simeon both recognized his divine charge.

Shortly after the Magi left, Herod became enraged because the Wise Men had not returned to tell him where the baby was located. Unbeknownst to Mary and Joseph, he issued his terrible decree that all male children aged two and under should be slaughtered.

An angel came to St. Joseph in a dream, and said, "Arise, and take the Child and His Mother, and fly into Egypt: and be there until I shall tell thee. For it will come to pass that Herod will seek the Child to destroy Him" (Matt. 2:13).

Rosalie Marie Levy writes, "We see that to Joseph, the Head of the Holy Family, was entrusted the charge of preserving the life of the Christ Child. To him, alone, would redound this privilege. While all men would contribute to the death of the Savior, only one, St. Joseph, was to save Him from death in His infancy."[211]

He had to take his young wife and their new baby one hundred and eighty miles to the pagan, unfamiliar country of Egypt. When they journeyed to Bethlehem, it was in their own familiar Jewish countryside, and they could travel leisurely by day. Now they had to flee at night, fearing for Jesus's life, into a land filled with danger and hostility toward people of their nationality and religion. Once again, Joseph asked no questions and made no protests. He simply obeyed.

After a lapse of time, some say six or seven years, an angel returned to Joseph in his sleep to tell him it was time to go home. They began the long journey back, and on the way, Joseph wondered if it was safe for them to return to the area around Bethlehem. He prayed and waited patiently for guidance.

The angel came to him in his sleep again and told him to take the Holy Family to Galilee. They settled in Nazareth. The prophets had foretold that Our Lord would be known as a Nazarene. We can imagine the peaceful silence and gentleness of the home life of the Holy Family. St. Joseph never yelled or showed irritability; Our Lady never complained of her many household chores; and the Christ child never showed the least sign of disrespect or disobedience to the wishes of His parents.

---

[211] Levy, 60.

We know that every year Jewish men journeyed to Jerusalem, and when Our Lord turned twelve, He was bound by the same law. On that particular trip, Joseph experienced another great trial of his patience and humility. Imagine his horror when he discovered that he had lost the Child entrusted to him? We know that he did nothing wrong, but he suffered nonetheless.

We can imagine poor tortured Joseph, with his arm around his weeping blessed wife, as they searched for three days. He thought he had failed as a protector and father. Maybe he even wondered if now was the time that the Child would die for all mankind? He did not know when the Passion and Death would come; he only knew that the prophets had foretold that it would.

When they finally found Him in the temple, Our Lady once again showed how she honored St. Joseph: "Behold *Thy father* and I have sought Thee sorrowing" (Luke 2:48, emphasis added). Imagine the relief they both felt! Our Lord hereby teaches us that when we lose Him (by sin), we can always find him in the Church.

After that, the next eighteen years are summed up in St. Luke's Gospel by the words, "And He went down with them, and came to Nazareth, and was subject to them . . . And Jesus advanced in wisdom, and age, and grace with God and men" (Luke 2:51–52). To our knowledge, St. Joseph never performed any miracles, preached any sermons, or worked any wonders. Yet he is considered the greatest saint after his pure wife Mary.

We have no account of his death, but he is not mentioned as being present at the Marriage Feast of Cana, or any other time in the public life of Our Lord. Rosalie Marie Levy points out that if Joseph were still alive at the Crucifixion, Our Lord would not have given His Mother to St. John.[212] She obviously must have been a widow at that time.

It takes very little imagination to picture the beautiful death of this faithful, just, kind, obedient saint. He slipped away gently, with Our Lord and Our Lady beside him to comfort him. Venerable Mary of Agreda says that he was sixty years old and had lived with Our Lady for twenty-seven years.

Tip for Phlegmatics: *The virtues of Joseph are the easiest for you to attain: patience, humility, and obedience. Do not let anyone tell you that these are not manly or courageous virtues—the life of St. Joseph proves otherwise.*

St. Bernard of Clairvaux, as quoted by Rosalie Marie Levy, says, "He was a faithful and prudent servant, I say, whom the Lord gave as a consolation to His Mother, as the guardian of His Own Body, and finally as the only and most faithful helper upon earth in the great plan of His Incarnation."[213]

After the death of St. Joseph, Our Lady carried on bravely without her faithful companion. She continued to assist her Son in His mission in every way she could. And her final words to us in the Gospel are: "Whatsoever He shall say to you, do ye" (Jn. 2:5). Therein lies the answer to our salvation, and the secret to holiness. We do what the Master tells us, in the doctrines, teachings and commandments of His Church, and in the innermost recesses of our hearts, when, with a well-formed conscience, we feel moved to think or act in accordance with His principles.

---

[212] Levy, 81.
[213] Levy, 28.

10

Discouragement & Depression by Temperament[214]

"Serve ye the Lord with gladness. Come in before His presence with exceeding great joy."

—Psalm 99:2

In the life of St. Paul, we talked about the good sadness that comes from being contrite for our sins: grieving for the passion and death of Our Lord and feeling heartache for Our Lord's sufferings that are caused by so many sins in the world. This kind of sadness is productive—it does not drag us down. It draws us onward and upward. It makes us want to do good, like peaceful protests outside abortion clinics or making a Holy Hour of reparation.

Bad sadness is the more common one, and we must assiduously avoid it. The devil, and our own fallen human nature, often cause us to drift into despair or depression, sadness or discouragement.

"The enemy [the devil] makes use of sadness to try the perseverance of the good," wrote St. Francis de Sales. "For, as he endeavors to rejoice the wicked in their sins, so he

[214] Disclaimer: If you have serious clinical depression or suicidal thoughts, be sure to seek help.

endeavors to sadden the just in their good works, and as he cannot draw them to evil unless by making them find it pleasant, so he cannot turn them away from good unless by making them find it wearisome."[215]

What a clever tempter Satan is! When he cannot get us to stop doing good, he makes it wearisome so that we want to give up on our own. Forewarned is forearmed.

How can we tell for sure if it is the bad sort of sadness, the destructive kind, the kind to flee from? St. Francis de Sales explains, "Bad sadness troubles the soul, throws it into uneasiness, inspires it with inordinate fears, and fills it with disgust for prayer; stupefies and confuses the brain; deprives the soul of counsel, resolution, judgment, courage, and entirely abases its powers."[216]

In other words, if all you want to do is hit the nearest bar for a whiskey and soda or take a spoon to a half-gallon of Rocky Road ice cream, you are probably not feeling the good sort of sadness. The bad sadness clouds our thinking, bogs us down, and makes us feel like not doing anything at all. The good sadness motivates us to perform good deeds and avoid sin.

Each temperament, and each person, is brought down by different causes. Cholerics are often depressed when things seem to be out of control, or they do not feel appreciated for all they do. Phlegmatics are discouraged when there is conflict and divisiveness. They just want everyone to get along. They also want to be appreciated for being who they are, even though they may not be the CEO, the party hostess, or the rocket

---

[215] de Sales, *Consoling Thoughts on Trials of an Interior Life*, 93–94.

[216] de Sales, 94.

scientist. Doesn't everyone want to be appreciated? The other two temperaments are even more prone to discouragement—the Sanguine, for a moment anyway, until something distracts him or her, and the Melancholic, who must battle it daily.

The Sanguine may seem very upbeat and happy all the time, but the changeable wind can blow in a sudden rain cloud on a gusty day. Under this cloud, the Sanguine feels that life is no fun and he or she is unloved. Sanguines want to be loved, to please others, and to know that others love them and are pleased by their antics, jokes, stories, and effusive affection.

People with other temperaments are shocked that a Sanguine is depressed when there is no fun to anticipate or when no one is giving him or her attention. "For goodness' sake, grow up!" they say to the Sanguine, making her shrink even more into herself and the darkness. This makes her feel more unloved, and that she should hide her true feelings and not tell others what is bothering her. God made all the four temperaments, and allowing the issues that are bothering us a legitimate means of escape from being bottled up inside us, is very salutary.

> ***Tip for Cholerics, Melancholics, and Phlegmatics:*** *Learn from the Sanguines how to serve with joy.*

A Sanguine does not want to do the job unless it is going to be fun—drudgery never appeals to him. But remember, God wants us to work toward having the *strengths* of all four temperaments.

Maybe it is going a little too far to say that God wants life to be fun, but He does tell us over and over in Scripture to live with joy, to sing with joy, to serve Him with joy. If there were no Sanguines in the world, there would be a lot more faux martyrs who drag themselves through life complaining and feeling sorry for themselves. God wants us to serve Him cheerfully, and the Sanguines show us how.

"Grant, we beseech Thee, O Lord, our God, that we, who in this life *joyfully* assist in the commemoration of Thy saints, may hereafter *rejoice* in beholding them forever in Heaven."[217] Holy Mother Church commands the priest to say this Postcommunion in the Common Mass for a martyr who was not a bishop. The Communion and Postcommunion are the prayers that the Church offers after Holy Communion at Mass.

The Sanguine does this celebratory giving by nature. They throw parties and run around making sure everyone is having fun because it comes to them naturally. God wants us to serve with joy and to bring others joy as well.

It is difficult, however, for anyone to be joyous or to bring joy to others when they are discouraged or depressed. Sanguines, of course, should try to control their desire for attention, but at the same time, they are usually warm and giving of themselves. They are happy to bring a basket of goodies to a sick person or invite over a friend who is going through a difficult time. Although a Sanguine needs and expects attention from others, the warmth and giving of his or her personality is the "bright side" of this. If we want to have the strengths of this temperament (whether we are Sanguine or not), we should try to be cheerful, even in adversity, and give affection and attention to others as an act of charity. St. Teresa of Ávila, who was part Sanguine, danced and sang with her Carmelite Sisters!

[217] Lasance, *The New Roman Missal*, 1312. Emphasis added.

When we are brought low, let us examine the reasons. First and foremost, it is usually the devil who brings sadness. He cannot bear to see us happy, and to know that we have the chance at everlasting happiness that he threw away, so he loves to drag us down. Discouragement is the shiniest instrument in his tool shed, they say.

"The devil *inflates* all the difficulties and at the same time *hides* that which renders the Christian life easy: flight from occasions of sin, prayer, the Sacraments, the profound joys of a Christian family, and eternal bliss," wrote Father Ludovic-Marie Barrielle.[218]

Tip for Discouraged Sanguines: Find someone to talk out your sadness with, and if possible, find a way to laugh about it!

Satan, ever the serpentine tempter, entangles himself around the nearest tree trunk and whispers to the Sanguine, "Nobody loves you. Nobody cares. Everything is just work, work, work. It's hopeless, it's miserable, it's not worth going on." He punctures the balloon of the Sanguine's joyous and bubbly natural optimism.

St. Ignatius says that the devil does not want us to speak out loud the things he whispers into our ears. As soon as the Sanguine talks out these awful thoughts with a confessor, spiritual director, or good Catholic friend, the venom dissipates. Sometimes Sanguines are even brought to laughter over the silliness of what upset them so much just a little while ago.

The Choleric has more trouble showing his or her weakness to anyone. Cholerics prefer to let out their steam in a rage, yelling and pounding the desk and calling everyone around them an idiot. Though a Choleric may seem domineering, he often is raging because he feels that he

[218] Barrielle, *Rules for Discerning the Spirits*, 9.

is not in control of the situation, or that he is unappreciated for all his accomplishments and leadership. Once again, the serpent is whispering to him, bringing unrest and discontent to his heart. The Choleric should find someone he respects (and there are many whom he does not respect) and listen attentively to that person's opinion of what is going on in his soul.

Tip for Discouraged Cholerics: Know thyself. Identify what is really dragging you down—are you unable to control people or situations around you? Are you feeling unappreciated? Sometimes the identification of the problem helps you to feel better.

It takes a long time for the Phlegmatic to build up to blowing his top or bursting into tears, but once he does, it's hard to pull him back out of it. He may not want to talk about it, but it is always good to expose the lies of the devil, and what he is using to destroy our peace of soul. Expose it to the open air and kill the infection that festers within.

"When one is in pain," wrote the Phlegmatic, Saint Thomas Aquinas, "It is natural that the sympathy of a friend should afford consolation . . . because, since sorrow has a depressing effect, it is like a weight whereof we strive to unburden ourselves: so that when a man sees others saddened by his own sorrow, it seems as though others were bearing the burden with him, striving, as it were, to lessen its weight; wherefore the load of sorrow becomes lighter for him: something like what occurs in the carrying of bodily burdens."[219] He goes on to say that the comfort and sympathy of our friends also makes us feel loved, which in turn encourages us.

---

[219] *ST* I–II. Q. 38. Art. 3.

This is a good place to point out the importance of choosing a good and salutary confidant. A female friend who tells a woman, "You're right. Your husband's a jerk. You should leave him," is doing more harm than good. That's not true sympathy, nor true friendship. The Irish use the phrase *anam cara*, or "soul friend." In ancient times, it meant your spiritual director—the one who is a friend to your soul. But our confidant, whether an ordained priest or a sibling or friend, should be a "friend to our soul:" one who truly loves us in the sense that they want what is best for our soul.

> ***Tip for Discouraged Phlegmatics:*** *Follow the example of St. Thomas Aquinas, and turn to a friend. Try to overcome your natural reticence, and tell them what's bothering you.*

If we do not choose a true *anam cara* to unburden ourselves to, we open ourselves to the possibility of the "therapy session" that deteriorates into pure gossip, complaining against the will of Almighty God, becoming angrier and more resentful toward others. Someone who is not a true friend to our soul can stoke the fires of our anger and desire for revenge, and other negative and harmful feelings. Instead, we should choose someone who is sensible, virtuous, and knowledgeable, someone whose judgment we trust, and who develops his or her mind by good reading.

Our Lord, in His terrible Agony in the Garden, did not unburden Himself to five hundred disciples. Instead, He chose three close friends—Peter, James, and John—and tried to show them how He really felt: His fear and terror at His upcoming passion, His heartbreak at the knowledge of those who would reject His offer of love and forgiveness, and the heavy burden of all the sins of the entire planet oppressing Him.

"One of the safest remedies is to discover our heart, without concealing anything, to some prudent and spiritual person," says St. Francis de Sales, "Mentioning to him the resentments, attachments, and suggestions that proceed from our sadness, and the reasons with which we entertain them; and all this humbly and faithfully. The first condition that the devil imposes on a soul which he wishes to afflict and seduce, is silence, just as the seditious do in conspiracies, for they require above all things that their undertakings and resolutions should be kept secret."[220]

This saint also says that a good walk with a friend is a cure for discouragement and sadness. Adding exercise to our choice of a good friend can also be helpful to alleviate downcast thoughts and feelings. Nowadays, many people run to relieve stress, whether in the fresh air or on a treadmill.

"If you have no other occupation, I would rather you should walk on the Mall," Bishop Landriot of La Rochelle told his ladies' society in the 1800s. The Mall was a place to walk along the seashore. "At all events, the sea air does good and expands the chest, whilst the atmosphere of some reveries causes physical and moral disease."[221] In other words, instead of brooding, get out and get some fresh air and exercise!

St. Thomas Aquinas says, "Sorrow, by reason of its specific nature, is repugnant to the vital movement of the body; and consequently whatever restores the bodily nature to its due state of vital movement, is opposed to sorrow and assuages it."[222]

---

[220] de Sales, *Consoling Thoughts on Trials of an Interior Life*, 110.
[221] Landriot, *The Valiant Woman*, 16.
[222] *ST* I–II. Q. 38. Art. 5.

He also recommends a good sleep and a bath, quoting St. Augustine as saying, "I had heard that the bath had its name from the fact of its driving sadness from the mind." He quotes the hymn of Saint Ambrose[223] thus: "Sleep restores the limbs to labor, refreshes the weary mind, and banishes sorrow."[224]

Besides the beauty of God's creation, and the natural gifts of sleep and refreshing water, He has also given us the gift of music to lift our spirits. If you cannot sing, listen to someone else's music that you admire! Many of today's songs, aside from the evils of certain rhythms and beats and screamed lyrics, are filled with sadness and pain. Does this drag us down, or lift us up? St. Francis de Sales especially recommends singing hymns and spiritual songs to lift our hearts. Who cares if you're off-key? Sing ye joyfully unto the Lord! "Sing joyfully to God, all the earth; make melody, rejoice and sing" (Ps. 97:4).

When you are in a relatively good mood, make a list of things to raise your spirits when you are down. Do you like photography? Baking? Working on or waxing your car? Window shopping? Make a list of things to do that will bring you joy so that you know what to do when you need a little refreshment.

Let's turn now to the Melancholics. Alas, the very name for Melancholics indicates that they are sad. And yet, Fr. Conrad Hock, in his book on the four temperaments, says that many of the saints were melancholic![225] Though we will hopefully find out for sure in Heaven how heavily those born with a

---

[223] Saint Ambrose (339–397).

[224] *ST* I–II. Q. 38. Art. 5. Cited therein as cf. *Sarum Breviary*: First Sunday after the octave of the Epiphany, Hymn for first Vespers.

[225] Hock, *The Four Temperaments*, 39.

Melancholic temperament are represented among the blessed, we all know that saints are not sad. Frank Sheed wrote a whole book with that title—over four hundred pages of accounts of joy-filled saints. So, if many of the saints were of a Melancholic temperament, and yet they were not sad, how is that possible?

They conquered their weakness, by the grace of God. They fought against what St. Francis de Sales refers to as "bad sadness." They rejoiced in their weakness being a reason for God to lift them above it. We may be inclined to alcoholism or kleptomania, but we do not have to abandon ourselves to these tendencies. Instead, we should find ways to fight back against our lower nature.

God told Saint Paul, "'My grace is sufficient for thee; for power is made perfect in infirmity'" (2 Cor. 12:9). And Paul continues, "Gladly therefore will I glory in my infirmities, that the power of Christ may dwell in me. . . . For when I am weak, then am I powerful" (2 Cor. 12:9, 10). Here is Saint Paul, a strong Choleric, admitting his weakness. We can see how grace worked on his heart after his conversion.

Did he mean that he wallowed in his weakness? Of course not! Can you imagine the strident, decisive Saint Paul wallowing? He fights temptation with all his strength—the thorn in his side he mentions in this epistle—but he also accepted that he was weak and could not win without God's help. Let us apply this to our sadness or discouragement.

We usually can see it coming. Melancholics become discouraged when they feel that things are not perfect. For this reason, they are more prone to sadness than the other temperaments. This life is not perfect! We are not perfect! Our spouses, children, classmates, co-workers, fellow religious, are not perfect! This *is* discouraging if we dwell on it.

> ***Tip for Melancholics:*** *Be vigilant—watch out for the dangers of discouragement before they get to you. Look out for them on the horizon. Life is not perfect, so they are often going to swoop in and try to steal your joy.*

This life is a ship and not a port, as Saint Thérèse is known to have said. These discouraging thoughts and happenings are only temporary. God is dependable, not the people or things in this life. Even our best friends or our spouses cannot always give us what we need. We must expect, as pessimistic Melancholics often do, that we cannot rely on this world to make us happy. The world *will* let us down; it's a fact of life. The prince of this world is Satan, and he is the greatest of all liars. The only way we will not be let down is if we put all our faith in God, not in people or in things. We should surround ourselves with people and things that are of God and put our trust in Him.

Melancholics have trouble hanging onto their hope. Hope tells us that there is a light at the end of this tunnel. Hope anchors our confidence that God is the one in control, that God wants us to give our best and leave the rest to Him.

"Our soul should also be provided with its anchor," writes Monseigneur Landriot, Archbishop of Rheims, "Nay, with many anchors suspended from the bulwarks; and when the storm comes, she [the soul] should drop them into the depths of God's providence, and rest unmoved, awaiting the end of the tempest." He names these anchors: "Good and well-established principles, great firmness of character, safe and pious friendships, and, above all, unshaken confidence in God, and energetic faith, capable of moving mountains."[226]

---

[226] Landriot, *The Valiant Woman*, 42.

> ***Tip for Discouraged Melancholics:*** *"Drop your anchor into the depths of God's Providence, and rest unmoved, awaiting the end of the tempest."*

Let's take a look at these anchors of hope in stormy waters. Archbishop Landriot mentions good and well-established principles and great firmness of character. A Choleric, no doubt, would say, well, at least I have those. But do we have the ones God wants us to have? Is our conscience rightly formed? Do I have principles based on God's law and my duties of state, or are my principles based on self-love and a desire to do it my own way or the way I see as the most organized, most perfect way? Let us be sure our anchor is a strong one, and not a crumbling bit of deception.

The same applies to firmness of character. A stone has firmness, but does a stone have virtue? We acquire the right kind of firmness through the grace of God. Let us not be stony-hearted or stiff-necked, as the Bible says, but rather, be valiant men and women of flesh and blood who have the charity of Our Lord in our hearts. Let our firmness come of virtue, and not of stubbornness. Let our "unshaken confidence" and "energetic faith" be in Almighty God Himself, and not the confidence or faith of pride in ourselves and our capabilities. Of ourselves, we are unable to do anything that is untainted with self-love and self-interest. Only by God's grace can we do anything virtuous. With God's grace, we can do all things in Him who strengthens us (see Phil. 4:13).

Archbishop Landriot also referred to good and pious friendships, which we have already covered. On the contrary side of this, of course, are the shaky, unreliable, unsupportive aspects of friendships that are not good and pious. They do not anchor our ship in the storms but cause us more distress and more difficulty. These are sinful friendships, worldly friendships, vainly flattering friendships with no purpose and no virtue. Let us avoid these and instead seek good Catholic companionship.

Perhaps Father Hock said that many of the saints were Melancholic because he saw the strengths of the Melancholic in so many of them. But that does not mean that it came to them naturally. They actively cultivated the virtues of the Melancholic temperament—desire for the highest ideal, persistence, attention to detail (as in, eradicating venial sins and faults), and taking time for silence. A Sanguine may not naturally take time for silence, but he or she can attain a desire for it, with God's grace.

> ***Tip for Sanguines, Cholerics, and Phlegmatics:*** *Learn from the Melancholics to desire the highest ideal, be persistent in eradicating your faults, and taking time for silence.*

For some people, a low point comes when anger is suppressed instead of legitimately vented. For others, it comes when we are around a certain person, or when something goes wrong at work, or any number of other triggers. Let us identify our triggers, and then reinforce our spiritual defenses in that area. Prayer, of course, is the first defense of all the temperaments.

In addition to consulting a soul friend, exercise, a good night's sleep, and a bath, St. Francis de Sales offers some other ideas. He says we should be patient when we see the sadness upon us. The Irish say that the sadness is "upon me" instead of saying, "I am sad." There is a subtle but essential difference. We are not the sadness. The sadness does not become who we are. The sadness is upon us, like a cloud that will waft away again on a breeze. St. Francis de Sales says that we should be patient, and not become alarmed or anxious or angry at the approach of discouragement, sadness, or frustration.

He says that if we are doing something good, keep doing it. The devil may very well be trying to make us sad to stop us from doing something good. We get more merit for good works when we do not feel like performing them, but act for the pure love of God anyway. He recommends acts of devotion, such as aspirations , kissing the crucifix, or other external movements of faith, hope, and love, *especially* if one does not feel like it.

Lastly, he recommends that if we have tried everything and we still cannot lift our mood, to simply anchor our hearts to the Cross and wait for the storm to pass. It will. Nothing could lift Mother Mary's spirits as she stood beneath the Cross on Calvary, but she waited patiently, uniting her sufferings to His, and then came the Resurrection and glorification of Her only Son beyond any mother's wildest dreams. God will glorify our souls forever in Heaven, if we hang on tightly to His will and to His Church, through the roughest storms and the worst sufferings, without self-pity, without wallowing. We must hang on for dear life to His Truth, which will set us free.

"The joyfulness of the heart is the life of a man, and a never-failing treasure of holiness: and the joy of a man is length of life. Have pity on thy own soul, pleasing God, and contain thyself: gather up thy heart in his holiness: and drive away sadness far from thee. For sadness hath killed many, *and there is no profit in it*" (Ecclus. 30:23–25).

11

Fear of Things to Come

One of the scourges of the last one hundred years or so is a fear that the end of the world is practically upon us. Saint Paul thought the same thing, and the world has hung on for another 2,000 years since then. We cannot say that the world *will not* come to an end soon, but no man knows the date nor the hour. No one can—even if they say they have had a revelation about it.

A Melancholic person may spend all of his or her time reading books of Catholic prophecy, taking apart the Book of the Apocalypse, worrying, and disturbing everyone around them. They might lose sleep, agonizing over stockpiling food for the end times, or scouring their conscience for things that will come out at the General Judgment. They might go around telling everyone that the world is coming to an end, frightening small children, and giving young people the idea that they will not reach maturity.

A Sanguine person may "freak out," running around in a state of frenzy thinking that everything is hopeless. He or she may flip the other way, and decide, "Eat, drink, be merry, for tomorrow we die!" Some Sanguines might abandon their principles because panic induces them to give up on trying to do God's will.

A Choleric person may be writing books on the end of the world, joining organizations to stockpile food for the terrible persecutions and trials that will come under the Antichrist, and ordering everyone around them to ignore his example at their own peril to body and soul.

The Phlegmatic is probably the least affected by worries of this kind. He usually does not see the point in getting all riled up about it. But he may secretly burrow into a deep part of himself, quietly worrying and silently letting it destroy his joy and peace.

As the world becomes worse and worse: politically, morally, and physically deteriorating, meteors coming, weather patterns changing, overall health declining, it is easy to get depressed about it all. But as a BBC poster says: "Greece is collapsing, Iranians are getting aggressive & Rome is in disarray. Welcome back to 430 BC!"[227]

Let us pray. Ask Our Lord to take us into His Heart and protect us from all the things that may happen in the world. If we are in His Heart, then we will have the strength to deal with whatever may happen. If we are in the state of sanctifying grace, and we take all reasonable measures to protect ourselves and our family from the moral and physical danger in the world, then there is no use worrying. Once again, God's timing is perfect. He knows the right time for each prophecy to be fulfilled, and some of them will not—they are just private revelations that people think will happen!

Our first priority is still to get to Heaven, whether we are hit by a truck this afternoon, or are still on earth at the Second Coming of Christ. It doesn't take a worldwide

---

[227] Quote is attributed to the English actor, John Cleese.

computer crash or a nuclear war for us to meet our Maker. We could fall down the stairs and break our neck tomorrow. Then the four Last Things will become the four immediate, all-important things—Death, Judgment, Heaven, and Hell.

It doesn't matter what the world is going to do or not going to do, we are still in the Palm of His Hand. We are still only responsible for what we *can* do, what we *can* control. Can I control what the president is doing? Can I control what the pope is doing? Can I control what the United Nations is doing? No, but I can control my own actions.

When it is time for my judgment, I need to be ready. In the depths of our souls, we need to be ready. How? By doing God's Will, by following His Commandments, by bringing others to His Light when we can. We need to do this whether the world is coming to an end this week, or 4,000 years from now.

If we pray the daily rosary, attend Mass and receive the Sacraments frequently, and remain in the state of sanctifying grace, then we are ready for whatever happens. Let us make Holy Hours in front of the Blessed Sacrament, let us take twenty minutes daily for contemplation of the life of Our Lord or meditation on spiritual subjects, and let us face the world while holding His Hand. This is the answer. This will save us. This will give us peace, now and in eternity.

Ode to Joy

"Joy lends wings to the soul."

—Fr. Almire Pichon, SJ[228]

All of us, regardless of temperament, are called to joy. "Rejoice in the Lord always; again, I say, rejoice" (Phil. 4:4). St. Paul makes it abundantly clear with these words: we are to rejoice *always*—Sanguines and Cholerics, Melancholics and Phlegmatics—both in consolations and in tribulations.

Maybe you are a natural Sanguine, and think, "It's okay to be happy? I've always been told to take life more seriously!" Maybe you are more Melancholic by nature, and think, "It's hard to look at the bright side when there is so much suffering and evil in this world!" Maybe as a Choleric, you look down on people who are too chipper or cheery and think they are irresponsible. Maybe as a Phlegmatic, you find it easier to flop on the sofa and drown your disappointments in binge-watching or a long nap. Again, I say, regardless of temperament, we are commanded by the all-loving God to rejoice.

"As to the rest, my brethren, rejoice in the Lord" (Phil. 3:1).

---

[228] Pichon, *Seeds of the Kingdom*, 225.

Father Almire Pichon, SJ, spiritual director to St. Thérèse of Lisieux, wrote, "My dear friends, you should thrill with joy, should fall upon your knees to send forth your *alleluias* of gratitude to the God who has accorded you the greatest of all graces—the grace to live in His love."[229] How blessed we are to have the gift of living in the state of grace, with so many celestial helps and so many heavenly friends cheering us on the path to eternal happiness!

The saints offer numerous ideas for cultivating joy in our lives, and Father Pichon offers another one. He says that if we truly love, we will respond to whatever happens with: "Amen (so be it), Deo Gratias (thanks be to God), Alleluia!" People who attended his retreats adopted this wonderful habit, and it spread among the faithful of his time. "Amen! Deo gratias! Alleluia!"

"Holy Indifference replies to suffering: Amen, I accept!" he wrote. "Holy Love cries out: Alleluia, Deo Gratias, I accept with joy!"[230]

We know that God has a perfect plan for us. When we cooperate, it brings us peace "which surpasseth all understanding" (Phil. 4:7) in this life, and eternal happiness with Him in the next. "The will of God must be our unique joy, our sole source of contentment,"[231] Father Pichon wrote.

We learned from the story of St. Peter that we should place all our confidence in God and His grace, not in ourselves. We "ought always to pray" (Luke 18:1), and we also have learned to place unlimited confidence in His will and in His infinite

---

[229] Pichon, 94.

[230] Pichon, 7.

[231] Pichon, 18.

care of us. The number of hairs on our head is known to Him; surely, He knows our needs (see Matt. 10:30).

When a father sees a child giggling and frolicking with glee because of the gifts she has been given, he smiles. How much more does our heavenly Father want to see us rejoice in all that He has done for us?

Father Pichon tells a story about Sanguine-Choleric St. Teresa of Ávila, in which she gave the Sisters an extra period of recreation on Easter Sunday. "St. Teresa of Ávila cultivated a spirit of joy in all of her monasteries," he writes. But one of the Sisters, a serious one, asked, "'Mother, would it not be preferable on Easter day to meditate rather than to make merry?'

"'Remain in your cell, if you wish,' replied the saint, 'but permit your sisters to rejoice, to expand their hearts in the Lord.'"[232]

Saint Teresa, who had the gift of actual conversations and mystical experiences with Our Lord, had learned that He wants to see us joyful. He knows that this life is hard, that we are suffering in this vale of tears, but He wants us to take time to rejoice in His goodness and His love.

Our Lord once told Teresa, "Do what lies in your power. Surrender yourself to Me and do not be disturbed about anything. Rejoice in the good that has been given you, for it is very great. My Father takes His delight in you and the Holy Spirit loves you."[233]

The Holy Ghost tells us in Scripture in the words of King David, "Come let us praise the Lord with joy: let us joyfully

---

[232] Pichon, 37.

[233] *Words of Hope*, 8.

sing to God our Saviour" (Ps. 94:1). Never once does God tell us in Scripture to worry, be anxious or stressed, or lose our peace of soul. Always He tells us to rejoice, to have courage, and to have peace.

How would your joy be filled if you took these words of Our Lord as your motto?
- *Do what lies in your power, then*
- *Surrender yourself to God.*
- *Do not be disturbed about anything,*
- *Rejoice in all the good God has done for you, and*
- *Know that you are infinitely loved.*

"These things I have spoken to you, that My joy may be in you, and your joy may be filled" (Jn. 15:11).

Fr. Pichon says that when we come before the judgment seat of God, we will think, "Oh, had I but known how Your Heart loved me, watched over me, I should never have experienced those useless fears, those discouragements!"[234] Let us not waste our precious lifetime worrying, but go forth joyfully to fulfill our mission in God's Love.

"Anything is possible to him who has confidence," wrote Father Pichon. "If you could but visualize all the possibilities that lie before you! Horizons so sweeping that they are lost to view. Enter upon this way of love and confidence! There you will find all joy, all peace of heart and mind."[235]

Father Pichon quotes another venerable priest, "'There must always be something that we do not understand, something that we do not will, in order to leave room for generosity, a generosity to be followed by joy,' said Père Pouleroye."[236] Our dear Lord blesses us when we are generous and loving. He *accepts* our service and our resignation when it is offered

---

234 Pichon, *Seeds of the Kingdom*, 54.
235 Pichon, 251–252.
236 Pichon, 139.

begrudgingly, but He is glorified when we "serve ye the Lord with gladness. Come in before His presence with exceeding great joy" (Ps. 99:2).

Bibliography

A Lapide, Cornelius. *The Personality of St. Paul.* Translated by the Daughters of St. Paul. St. Paul Editions, 1979.

Alberione, James and T.M. Giaccardo. *A Month with Saint Paul.* The Daughters of St. Paul, 1952.

A Little White Flower: The Story of Saint Therese of Lisieux. A revised translation of the definite Carmelite edition of her autobiography, by the Rev. Thomas N. Taylor. P.J. Kenedy and Sons: NY, 1927.

Anderdon, W.H. *Afternoons with the Saints.* Burns and Oates: London, 1874.

Aquinas, Thomas. *Summa Theologica of St. Thomas Aquinas.* Translated by the Fathers of the English Dominican Province. Christian Classics: Westminster, MD, 1948.

Auclair, Marcelle. *Saint Teresa of Avila.* Translated by Kathleen Pond. Pantheon: NY, 1953. https://archive.org/details/saintteresaofavila_202002/mode/2up.

Augustine, *The Confessions of Saint Augustine, Books I–X.* Translated by F.J. Sheed. Sheed & Ward: New York, 1942.

Barrielle, Ludovic-Marie. *Rules for Discerning the Spirits.* Angelus Press: Kansas City, 1992.

Bougaud, Emile. *St. Chantal and the Foundation of the Visitation,* two volumes. Benziger Brothers, New York, Cincinnati: Chicago, 1895.

Brennan, Richard. *A History of the Catholic Church* or *Christ in His Church.* From the original of Rev. L.C. Businger. Benziger Brothers: New York, Cincinnati, Chicago, 1884.

Cassidy, James F. *St. Francis de Sales: The Doctor of Devotion.* M.H. Gill and Son, Ltd.: Dublin, 1945.

Chautard, Jean-Baptiste. *The Soul of the Apostolate*. Translated by a monk of Our Lady of Gethsemani. TAN Books and Publishers: IL, 1974.

Collins, Henry. *Heaven Opened; or, Our Home in Heaven and the Way Thither: A Manual of Guidance for Devout Souls*. Thomas Richardson & Son: London,1880.

Consoling Thoughts on Trials of an Interior Life. Gathered and arranged by Rev. Pere Huguet. TAN Books: Charlotte, NC, 2013.

Croiset, Jean. *The Devotion to the Sacred Heart of Our Lord Jesus Christ*. Translated by Rev. Patrick O'Connell. Reprinted by the International Institute of the Heart of Jesus: Milwaukee, 1976.

de Ligouri, Alphonsus, St. *The Love of Our Lord Jesus Christ Reduced to Practice: From the Words of St. Paul Addressed to Those Souls that are Anxious to Secure their Eternal Salvation, and to Advance Towards Perfection*. James Duffy and Sons: Dublin, 1841.

de Sales, Francis. *Introduction to the Devout Life*. Translated and edited by John K. Ryan. Image Books: NY, 1960.

Donnelly, Francis P. *The Heart of the Gospel: Traits of the Sacred Heart*. Apostleship of Prayer: NY, 1913.

Galy, A. *The Friend of Sinners*. Translated from the French by Rev. J.M. Lelen. Burns, Oates & Washbourne, Ltd: London, 1930.

Gilli, Gaspar. *The Month of Mary, According to the Spirit of St. Francis of Sales*. Translated and abridged from the Italian by a Sister of the Institute of Charity. St. Pius X Press: San Bernardino, CA, 2013.

Hallack, Cecily. *Wonder Worker: Saint Philomena, Virgin Martyr*. Anthonian Press: Dublin, 1945.

Hallett, Philip Edward. *Saint Thomas More*. Catholic Truth Society: London, 1955.

Heuser, Herman J. *The House of Martha at Bethany*. Longmans, Green & Co.: NY, 1928.

Hock, Conrad. *The Four Temperaments*. Revised and enlarged by Rev. Nicholas M. Wilwers, S.A.C., M.A. Catholic Apostolate Press: Milwaukee, WI, 1962.

Houselander, Caryll. *The Risen Christ*. Sheed & Ward: London, 1958. (Recommended for adults only)

Lacordaire, Pere H.D. *St. Mary Magdalen*. Translated by E.A. Hazeland. Burns and Oates: London, and Catholic Publication Society Co.: NY, 1880.

Lallemant, Louis. *The Spiritual Doctrine of Father Louis Lallemant of the Society of Jesus*. Newman Book Shop: Westminster, MD, 1946.

Landriot, Jean-François-Anne-Thomas. *The Valiant Woman: A Series of Discourses Intended for the Use of Women Living in the World*. Translated from the French by Helena Lyons. Loreto Publications: NH, 2005.

Lasance, F.X. *The New Roman Missal*. Christian Book Club of America: Palmdale, CA, 1993.

Levy, Rosalie Marie. *Joseph the Just Man*. Daughters of St. Paul, 1955.

Lewis, David. *Saint Teresa*. Catholic Truth Society: London, 1926.

Littauer, Florence. *Personality Plus*. Fleming H. Revell: Grand Rapids, MI, 2001.

———. *Your Personality Tree*. Word Publishing: Dallas, London, Vancouver, Melbourne, 1986.

Lloyd, Teresa. *A Child's Life of Blessed Thomas More*. Catholic Truth Society: London, 1930.

Massmann, Joseph. *Nervousness, Temperament and the Soul*. Roman Catholic Books: Fort Collins, CO, 1941.

Maurus, Rabanus. *The Life of St. Mary Magdalene and of Her Sister Saint Martha*. Translated and annotated by David Mycoff. Cistercian Publications: Kalamazoo, MI, 1989.

McGerr, Patricia. *Martha, Martha*. Dell Publishing: NY, 1960.

McNabb, Vincent. *St. Mary Magdalen.* O.P. Burns, Oates & Washbourne: London, 1940.

Minor Works of St. Teresa: Conceptions of the Love of God, Exclamations, Maxims and Poems of Saint Teresa of Jesus. Translated from the Spanish by the Benedictines of Stanbrook. Revised with notes and an introduction by the Rev. Fr. Benedict Zimmerman, O.C.D. Thomas Baker: London, 1913.

Morton, J.B. *St. Therese of Lisieux: The Making of a Saint.* Clonmore & Reynolds: Dublin, 1954.

Mullany, Katherine F. *Miriam of Magdala: A Study.* Magdala Company: NY, 1906.

O'Sullivan, Paul. *Saint Philomena the Wonder-Worker.* The Catholic Printing Press: Lisbon, 1954.

Pichon, Almire. *Seeds of the Kingdom: Notes from Conferences, Spiritual Directions, Meditations.* Edited by Lyle Terhune, T.O.C.D. Lepanto Press, 1961.

Plus, Raoul. *Christ in the Home.* Frederick Pustet Co., Inc.: 1951. https://archive.org/details/ChristInTheHomePart1.

Roche, Aloysius. *A Bedside Book of Saints.* Bruce Publishing Company: Milwaukee, 1934.

Rohrbach, Peter Thomas. *Conversation with Christ.* TAN Books: Charlotte, NC, 2010.

Seton, E. *Sundays in the Garden of Easter.* Burns, Oates & Washbourne Ltd.: Manchester, Birmingham, Glasgow, 1921.

Sheed, Frank J. *Saints are Not Sad.* Ignatius Press: San Francisco, CA, 2012.

Undset, Sigrid. *Catherine of Siena.* Translated by Kate Austin-Lund. Ignatius Press: San Francisco, CA, 2009.

Vaughan, Roger. *The Life and Labours of St. Thomas of Aquin.* Abridged and edited with preface by Dom Jerome Vaughan. Burns & Oates: London, 1890.

Words of Hope. Edited by Craig Turner. TAN Books: Charlotte, NC, 2014.